Estate Planning Fundamentals

Steven M. Bragg

AccountingTools®

ISBN 978-1-64221-314-0

For more information about AccountingTools® products, visit our Web site at www.accountingtools.com.

Table of Contents

About the Author

Steven Bragg, CPA, has been the chief financial officer or controller of four companies, as well as a consulting manager at Ernst & Young. He received a master's degree in finance from Bentley College, an MBA from Babson College, and a Bachelor's degree in Economics from the University of Maine. He has been a two-time president of the Colorado Mountain Club, and is an avid alpine skier, mountain biker, and certified master diver. Mr. Bragg resides in Centennial, Colorado. He has written more than 300 books and courses, including *New Controller Guidebook*, *GAAP Guidebook*, and *Payroll Management*. He has also written the science fiction novel *Under an Autumn Sun*, first book in *The Auditors* trilogy.

Steven maintains the accountingtools.com web site, which contains continuing professional education courses, the Accounting Best Practices podcast, and thousands of articles on accounting subjects.

Chapter 1
Your Estate Planning Goals

Introduction

Estate planning is all about transferring assets to other parties. Its goal is to do so while balancing tax efficiency and the needs of the disbursing and receiving parties. In this chapter, we discuss the various issues that can impact your estate planning goals.

Issues Impacting Estate Planning

There are numerous issues that can impact your estate planning goals. The following bullet points indicate the range of issues that may arise:

- Dividing property unequally between children
- Assigning rights to heirloom assets
- Dealing with grasping children
- Providing care for minors
- Providing care for disabled children
- Dealing with issues arising from second marriages

It is essential to recognize these issues as part of the estate planning process. If you do not, then there is a good chance that the outcome will be strife between those who received assets from your estate and those who did not (or who received less).

EXAMPLE

Donna and Allen have five children, of whom Charles is the obvious choice as executor. He is a CPA, and is routinely involved in fiduciary accounting. However, he has long indicated a desire to own Donna and Allen's home once they die. To keep Charles from having undue influence over how the house is assigned, they appoint the three oldest children as co-executors, where the majority vote decides how to apportion assets. Charles is one of the three designated executors, so he still has some say in the matter.

EXAMPLE

Evan has accumulated a large library of first edition mountaineering books, which his four children have obsessively read through their childhood years. All four want to keep these books after he dies. In order to avoid conflict later on, Evan arranges for the family to meet at his home, where the children are allowed to dicker over who gets what. Evan then incorporates their decisions into his will.

EXAMPLE

Maggie is 90 years old and owns a massive collection of valuable early American artwork. She is a multi-millionaire. She has been estranged from her son – a greedy and grasping individual – for years. She intends to leave her entire estate to a favorite art museum. To minimize the risk that her son will contest this arrangement, she hires the best law firm in town to construct an iron-clad will that he cannot breach.

EXAMPLE

Henry and Samantha have provided extra funding to their son Arnie, to whom they gave $250,000 to start up a new business. They decide to leave an extra $250,000 to their other son Douglas, who has not asked for such funding. By doing so, they believe they are being fair to both sons. They attach a letter to their will, explaining their reasoning for taking this approach.

EXAMPLE

Robin and George married later in life, and own a home together. Robin has three sons, while George has two daughters. To provide for their children, they decide to split the value of the house equally upon their deaths, with half of the value going to Robin's three sons and the other half going to George's two daughters.

EXAMPLE

Maria and Chris have three children, of which one is developmentally disabled and needs continual care. They decide to leave 80% of their estate to the disabled child in a special needs trust, splitting the remainder between the other two children. Their intent is to ensure that their disabled child is properly looked after. In addition, they appoint a financial guardian who will be responsible for ensuring that the funds allocated to the disabled child are properly used.

A variation on this concept is setting up a trust for any child who has difficulty handling money, with a trustee who must approve disbursements from the trust.

EXAMPLE

Terry has built up a substantial fortune through his startup business, and is concerned that his early-20s children would quickly dissipate the funds through unwise expenditures. Accordingly, he sets up a trust that pays out one quarter of the inheritance to the children every ten years. He believes that this incremental approach will keep the children reasonably secure through most of their lives.

EXAMPLE

Allison and Henry have a substantial estate, as well as a successful entrepreneur daughter who has built up a considerable fortune of her own. They decide to leave the bulk of their estate to a charity that works in an area that is important to both of them, leaving a modest sum for their daughter. They have a discussion with their daughter about this, so that she will not be surprised when the disbursements are eventually made.

When making any estate planning decisions, it is advisable to discuss the matter with those who expect to receive funds from your estate. Doing so may uncover issues or expectations that you were not aware of, which may alter your plans. Or, if your intent is to proceed without any changes, then this additional information may cause you to leave behind a letter to your heirs, explaining your thinking in making various distributions.

Tip: It can be useful to discuss the matter with close friends, who are in a good position to offer advice as uninterested parties.

Property Ownership Rules

Your estate planning goals may be heavily impacted by state-level property ownership laws that may give your spouse the right to claim a portion of your property in the event of your death. The situation depends on whether you live in a state that uses community property law, or one that uses common law. The states that use community property law are Arizona, California, Idaho, Louisiana, Nevada, New Mexico, Texas, Washington, and Wisconsin. All other states use common law. In a community property law state, spouses share property ownership, even if only one spouse's name is listed on a property title document. In this situation, each spouse has the right to leave their portion of the property to whomever they want, and have no control over how the other half is used. Conversely, in a common law state, the owner of an asset is the spouse whose name appears on the title document. However, common law states mandate that each spouse has a certain minimum claim on the assets of their partner at the other person's death, even if he or she left it to another party.

Tip: Given the differences in property ownership rules by state, you should clarify which state you are officially domiciled in. This is important in cases where you have residences in multiple states. If this is a gray area, consult with an attorney.

The ownership of property is based on the laws of the state in which the property is located, irrespective of your official state of residence.

It is possible to override the property laws of the state in which you are domiciled by creating either a prenuptial (prior to marriage) or postnuptial (after marriage) agreement. This is a contract that states how all property shall be owned. The terms of these contracts must be in accordance with local state law, which usually mandates that they be in writing and involve the full disclosure of the assets and liabilities of both parties.

Community Property Law Issues

The essential rule of community property law is that the property acquired or earned by each spouse during marriage is owned equally by each – which means that each one owns a half-share in it. An exception is any property received by just one of them through an inheritance or a gift. Another exception is any property owned by a spouse prior to the marriage, as long as it continues to be kept separate. When spouses have been married for a long time, there are rarely any assets left from before the marriage, either because they have been disposed of or mixed in with the couple's other assets. The following are considered to be community property:

- The income earned by either spouse during the marriage, though it is possible to enter into an agreement to keep their income as separate property; if so, it should be stored in separate bank accounts.
- The property purchased using community property income. For example, if you buy a motorcycle with your wages, the motorcycle is considered community property, even if your name is the only one stated on the title.
- Any separate property converted into community property. A spouse may agree in writing to gift separate property to both spouses, or through the commingling of assets, where assets are so mixed together that it is impossible to tell who owns what.

EXAMPLE

Ian had $100,000 in a checking account prior to his marriage. He has subsequently maintained the account through 10 years of marriage, but there have been so many deposits to and withdrawals from the account involving community transactions that the original $100,000 has become commingled with the pair's community property.

Under community property law, the following property is considered to be separate property:

- Any property that was owned by either spouse prior to their marriage
- Any property received by either spouse following the marriage date from an inheritance or gift
- Any property earned by either spouse once they have been permanently separated

Pensions have a somewhat different treatment under community property law. They are generally considered to be community property, but the benefits received from certain federal pension plans, such as social security, are considered to be the separate property of the recipient.

Another area that can cause trouble in differentiating assets is when both spouses contribute to the cost of maintaining an asset (such as a house) that is the separate property of just one of them. In this case, a portion of the value of the asset will now be considered community property.

Or, what happens if one person owns a business and then enters into a marriage? Disputes can arise over whether the subsequent growth of the business is now community property. If it is reasonable that most of the subsequent business growth would have occurred without the participation of the person's spouse, then an argument can be made that the spouse who originally owned the business continues to own its entire value. In this situation, the spouses can enter into an agreement to divide the value of the business in whatever manner they choose.

There are no restrictions on the manner in which each spouse may elect to leave his or her portion of any community property. Many spouses choose to leave their assets to their surviving spouse, but there is no requirement to do so.

Common Property Law Issues

Common property laws take a significantly different approach from community property law, because there is no rule that property obtained during marriage is owned by both spouses. Instead, its default condition is that a spouse who earns money and acquires property gets to own it. Evidence of this ownership can be any legal ownership document. The overriding rule is that evidence of ownership represents ownership of the underlying asset. Thus, if one spouse earns the money to buy a new car, but her husband's name is on the title to the car, then he owns the car. Clearly, both spouses must ensure that both of their names are included on all ownership documents, to ensure that they own an equal share of all assets. This situation could result in one spouse owning most (or all) of the assets. To prevent a surviving spouse from essentially being disinherited by this situation, all common property law states have enacted spousal inheritance laws that grant the survivor anywhere from one-third to one-half of the property of the other spouse. However, this property is not automatically granted – the surviving spouse needs to claim it in court. In essence, the surviving spouse can either elect to take what was provided for him or her in the decedent's will, or reject it and pursue the minimum share to which he or she is entitled under state law.

EXAMPLE

Ellen, a famous author, dies; her will leaves $5,000,000 to her daughter from an earlier marriage, $4,000,000 to her favorite charity, and $1,000,000 to her second husband, Edward. Edward has the choice of either taking the $1,000,000, which is 10% of Ellen's estate, or pursuing his statutory 1/3rd share of her estate. He elects to pursue the 1/3rd share, which amounts to $3,333,333. The extra $2,333,333 that he will receive must be subtracted from the distributions that would have gone to Ellen's daughter and favorite charity.

Tip: Since the surviving spouse in a common property state can greatly reduce the share of the decedent's estate going to other parties, it can make sense to set up the will to provide your spouse with the state-mandated minimum share of the estate. By doing so, you can ensure that the other beneficiaries will receive the amounts intended for them.

Tip: If you plan to move from a community property law state to a common property law state – or vice versa – verify what the impact of this change will be on how your estate is distributed.

Itemizing Your Property

A key part of estate planning is to create a detailed listing of your property. It can be used as the basis for a valuation of your estate, as well as to calculate the full amount of your liabilities. It is also a useful way to spot any instances of shared asset ownership. This itemization is especially useful when you plan to divide assets among several beneficiaries. Conversely, if you plan to leave your assets to just one person, then an asset itemization is less necessary.

EXAMPLE

Sarah has a number of hobbies, and has accumulated multiple assets related to each one. She wants to ensure that each set of assets is assigned to the correct beneficiary. Consequently, she creates an inventory of the 52 western historical paintings she has purchased, which will go to a regional western art museum. She also creates an inventory of the Indian pottery artifacts that she purchased from several estate sales in New Mexico, which will go to a pottery museum in that state. She does not bother to inventory anything else, since the remainder of her estate will go to her niece Kathleen.

The best way to itemize your property is in a grid pattern, with different types of property listed down the left side. Across the top of the grid are three columns, which are a brief description of the asset, the percentage of each asset that you own, and the value of your share of the asset. Further comments concerning the top of the grid are as follows:

1. *Property description.* The property description should be sufficiently detailed that each asset is clearly identified. For example, the account number associated with a 401(k) pension account should be stated, while the address for a vacation property should be listed. If you own undeveloped land for which there is no address, then state its location as best you can, such as the township within which it is located. Or, the number of shares you hold in a corporation should be stated, as well as the type of shares and the manner in which they are held (such as through a brokerage). If you are gifting property and any personal property on the premises, then say so – such as "my property at 123 Main Street, along with all personal property located there."

2. *Percentage of asset owned.* Some of your assets may be jointly owned with other parties. If so, research how much of them you own, and identify who else is an owner, in case your beneficiaries need to contact them. The percentage of asset ownership should be documented even when the other party is your spouse, as long as a third party (*not* your spouse) is the intended recipient. There are several types of shared ownership that might be associated with an asset. The most common ones are as follows:

    o   Community property. In a state that recognizes community property, any income and real or personal property acquired by either spouse during a marriage is considered community property and so belongs to both partners in the marriage. This means that both spouses own everything equally, no matter who earns or spends the income. You can leave your half of community property to any party, not necessarily your spouse.

- o Corporation shares. This arrangement gives you an ownership interest in a corporation, in the form of shares. The ability to transfer ownership of these shares may be restricted, depending on any associated shareholders' agreement.
- o Joint tenancy. Under this arrangement, each owner owns an equal share of the property. When the first owner dies, that person's share goes to the survivors. It must be created via a written document.
- o Limited liability company. This arrangement combines several aspects of partnerships and corporate ownership. The ability to transfer an ownership interest will likely be addressed by the entity's operating agreement.
- o Partnership. This arrangement covers property owned by a set of business partners, as covered by a partnership agreement. This agreement may cover what happens to each partner's ownership interest in the event of his or her death. It is common for other business partners to have the right to purchase your interest in the partnership.
- o Separate property. In a state that recognizes separate property, any property not identified as community property is held by a specific party.
- o Tenancy by the entirety. This arrangement is similar to joint tenancy, and gives the surviving spouse the entire ownership interest. It must be created via a written document.
- o Tenancy in common. Under this arrangement, several parties share ownership rights in a real estate property or parcel of land, where each owner controls a percentage of the total property. A tenancy in common has no right of survivorship, so when an owner dies, his or her share of the property passes to their estate, where it will be passed to a beneficiary.

3. *Net value of ownership.* This column contains the market value of your ownership interest in each asset, reduced by your share of any associated debts. For example, if the market value of your share in a residence is $800,000 and you are also liable for $200,000 of the associated mortgage, then the net value of ownership on that residence is $600,000. It is not necessary to pay for appraisals – the intent is only to write down your best guess at market values. A higher degree of accuracy is not necessary, since these asset values will likely change over time.

EXAMPLE

Franklin owns a vacation cabin with a market value of $250,000 under a tenancy in common arrangement with his neighbor Jonathan. Franklin and Jonathan each own half of the cabin. The total mortgage amount outstanding on the cabin is $100,000. This means that the total equity in the property is $150,000, of which Franklin and Jonathan each own $75,000.

There are numerous categories of assets and liabilities into which you might consider aggregating your assets. In the following subsections, we describe them further.

Liquid Assets

A liquid asset is any asset that is readily convertible into cash within a short period of time, and which suffers no loss in value as a result of the conversion. Convertibility is assisted by the presence of a large market in which there are many participants, and in which it is easy to transfer ownership from the buyer to the seller. Examples of liquid assets are cash, certificates of deposit, savings accounts, checking accounts, money market accounts, tradable securities, and precious metals.

Digital Assets

You may have substantial digital assets, such as domain names, websites, social media accounts, and email accounts. Or, even if they have little value, you should at least consider how these items should be dispositioned. For example, you might want to have someone close your Amazon account, terminate your email accounts, and transfer a family blog to someone else who is interested in preserving the family history. To ensure that these actions are taken, specify who is responsible for each task, and leave them the relevant user ID and password. Without this access information, it may take your executor a substantial amount of time to gain access permission from the online platforms on which these digital assets are housed.

One digital asset that may be worth a great deal of money is an online store. If you operate one, then leave complete instructions about how to access the store, where its domain name is registered, and how to update all related credit card information needed to continue operating the store. This might represent your single most important asset – if so, be sure to leave a thoroughly-documented operations manual.

Another digital asset that may be worth a substantial amount is cryptocurrency. The valuations of these currencies fluctuate wildly, so do not assume that something that currently has a minimal value is not worth documenting for a beneficiary – its value may increase substantially over time. If you have crypto currency holdings, document exactly where they are stored, along with the relevant access codes.

Other Personal Property

Personal property includes any asset other than real estate, liquid assets, and digital assets. The main difference between personal property and real estate is that personal property is movable; thus, it is not affixed permanently to one location. Property usually included within this category are automobiles, computers, household goods, clothes, jewelry, collectibles, and tools. It also includes any vested interests in profit sharing plans and pension plans, as well as the cash surrender value of life insurance policies.

> **Tip:** If you want to leave your frequent flier miles to a beneficiary, a good way to do so is to leave that person your login credentials, thereby giving the person immediate access to your miles.

> **Tip:** Do not itemize assets with minimal values. For example, if you have a large stamp collection and none of the stamps within it are valuable, then just state "stamp collection located in the study."

Real Estate

Real estate is likely to be your largest asset, so put the most effort into identifying these assets, specifying the extent of your ownership interest, and the amount of any offsetting mortgages. Given the size of these assets, this is the area of your asset listing most worthy of a regular update.

> **Tip:** If you plan to gift someone property that is contaminated, be aware that the beneficiary will take on the cost of decontamination, which may be greater than the value of the property. Therefore, it is best to ascertain whether contaminants are present before gifting property.

Business Property

If you own a business, then your ownership interest in it may well be the largest asset you own. However, it can be difficult to put a value on an operating business. One approach is to break the business down into its constituent parts and value each part separately. For example, you could assign a separate value to each patent, copyright, or trademark held. You could also assign values to specific contracts held by your business. Another option is to assign a value based on the cash flows generated by the business. Generally, the latter approach gives the best view of the value of the business to potential acquirers.

Liabilities

If any debts were not already accounted for within the earlier asset listings (usually as offsetting mortgages), then list them in this section. There are a variety of possibilities, such as an advance on a line of credit, a loan payable to an acquaintance, or a bank loan. Also, if there are court judgments against your estate or tax liens against your assets, then list them here. Do not bother to list incidental and ongoing liabilities, such as your utility bill or credit card charges.

Net Worth

This final section is a simple calculation, where you subtract all liabilities from all assets to arrive at a positive or negative net worth figure.

Summary

It can be useful to jot down your estate planning goals and make adjustments to this preliminary list, based on specific issues within your designated group of beneficiaries. Discussing these issues with uninvolved third parties can be a useful way to clarify how your gifts will impact the group, and what types of tensions may arise within the group as a result of these gifts. Before finalizing any estate planning documentation, let these issues simmer for a period of time, so that you can decide upon the best ways to deal with them. In short, deriving estate planning goals tends to be a moderately lengthy process.

Chapter 2
Beneficiary Issues

Introduction

A beneficiary is a person or entity that is designated to receive the benefits of property owned by someone else. When devising an estate plan, it is useful to understand the different types of beneficiaries, as well as several legal issues relating to them. We cover these topics in the following pages.

Types of Beneficiaries

There are several types of beneficiaries to whom you might leave your estate. The main focus of your estate planning will be *primary beneficiaries*, who are those parties to whom you are leaving identified gifts. If primary beneficiaries are unable to receive these gifts, then alternate beneficiaries are identified. The designation of alternate beneficiaries is especially useful when the primary beneficiaries are not in good health. There are several variations on these concepts. One is the *life estate beneficiary*, who receives the right to use an asset or receive income from it during his or her lifetime, but who will not be its legal owner. After a life estate beneficiary dies, the related asset goes to a *final beneficiary*, who inherits the property outright. Finally, there are *residuary beneficiaries*, who receive assets that have not been specifically gifted to other beneficiaries.

> **Tip:** Consider naming alternate beneficiaries, in case your primary beneficiaries die.

EXAMPLE

Sarah leaves her aunt Andrea a life estate interest in her house, where Andrea already lives. Sarah also names her son Robert to be the final beneficiary. This means that Andrea has use of the house during her lifetime, after which Robert inherits the house.

When you name a primary beneficiary, that person will receive a specific asset. For example, you might leave your vacation home to your son Philip. Alternatively, you might name no primary beneficiaries at all, in which case your entire estate will be left to your residuary beneficiaries.

> **Tip:** If you are planning to leave substantial assets to a minor, be aware that state law limits the amount that can be directly controlled by a minor to quite a small sum – usually just a few thousand dollars. It will be necessary to name an adult who will be responsible for administering the funds.

It is possible to gift assets to a primary beneficiary that imposes certain restrictions. For example, your son might be gifted a substantial amount of cash if he first completes college. These restrictions must be clearly defined, so that there is no question about when the beneficiary will inherit the related asset. For example, would your son receive the cash if he were to complete a two-year degree at a community college, or only if he were to complete a four-year degree?

> **Tip:** Most state governments do not allow you to enforce specific types of conduct by your beneficiaries. For example, a requirement for a daughter to divorce her husband as a condition of inheritance cannot be enforced.

A common gift for a primary beneficiary is the cancellation of a debt. For example, if you loaned someone $20,000, that person will be obligated to pay your estate after you die. However, if you specify that the debt is to be forgiven, then this constitutes a gift, since the net effect is to reduce the size of your estate.

It is a good idea to name a residuary beneficiary, who receives all property that will not be received by other named beneficiaries. This is especially important when there is a risk that the primary or alternate beneficiaries might die before you die. In essence, the residuary beneficiary is your Plan B, in case your primary option does not happen.

EXAMPLE

Steven and Josephine create a will, in which they leave their estate to their children. The entire family has paid for tickets on a sub-orbital flight, for which there is a non-zero risk of explosion and death for the family. In the hopefully unlikely event of the demise of everyone, Steven and Josephine designate their favorite charity as the residuary beneficiary of their estate.

Their favorite charity is a small one, and is at some risk of closing. To ensure that their estate is left in safe hands, Steven and Josephine designate a second (and much larger and more stable) charity as their alternate residuary beneficiary.

A common gift is for an asset to be left to several beneficiaries. If so, the beneficiaries are each given an ownership interest in the asset. This approach differs from having the asset sold first, with the funds being distributed among the beneficiaries. Instead, the beneficiaries now share ownership of the asset, and so must decide amongst themselves what to do with it.

EXAMPLE

Elinor leaves her home to her five children, with each child receiving a 20% ownership interest in the home. As a group, they decide to rent out the home and share the proceeds, rather than selling it.

Tip: If you plan to leave an asset to several beneficiaries, the assumption will be that each one is given an equal ownership share. If that is not the case, then specify who receives what percentages in your will. It can help to state that ownership shares will be distributed equally among the beneficiaries, to minimize squabbling.

The Survivorship Period Clause

It can be useful to include a survivorship period in your will. This is the amount of time that must pass following your death before the beneficiary can inherit. By setting a survivorship period, you can increase the odds that the designated assets will be gifted to your designated alternate beneficiary, in case the beneficiary dies soon after you do. Otherwise, the assets will be transferred into the beneficiary's estate, and from there to the beneficiaries selected by that party – which may be quite different from the recipients that you want.

Tip: A survivorship period of a few months is a reasonable duration when this clause is included in a will. However, it is not normally used in a living trust, where the intent is to shift assets to the beneficiaries as soon as possible.

The No-Contest Clause

A no-contest clause states that any beneficiary who sues to claim more than you specifically left them will lose all inherited assets if their claim is unsuccessful. Consider adding this clause when there is a risk that someone might conduct a challenge on the grounds that you were unduly influenced or incompetent when you created the will or trust. Typically, the clause is only necessary if the distribution of assets will leave a beneficiary feeling deprived of his or her "fair share".

The Simultaneous Death Clause

A simultaneous death clause states that, when it is difficult to determine which spouse died first, the property of each spouse is disposed of as though that person was the surviving spouse. The result is that each spouse's estate is handled separately, as though there is no other spouse. By doing so, each spouse can distribute his or her share of the estate in the manner they want. Otherwise, all assets might pass to your spouse (assuming this person is the survivor), and then passes to your spouse's beneficiaries – rather than your beneficiaries.

Explanations for Beneficiaries

It may be worthwhile to provide a written explanation for your designations of beneficiaries, as well as the ownership percentages given to them. Otherwise, there is some risk of hurt feelings among your beneficiaries. The following example illustrates how these differences can be explained.

EXAMPLE

Martha leaves the following explanation in her will:

> "I leave the value of my house to my three daughters, Sarah, Mikah and Gail. The share given to Mikah shall be $200,000 less than the shares given to her sisters, on the grounds that I have already given her this amount as ongoing support, as well as to pay for several cars and the down payment on her condominium."

Tip: An explanation included in a will becomes a public document, so instead consider attaching it to the will as a separate document.

Disinheritance

The only person who is entitled to your assets is your spouse, if you live in a common law state. Also, depending on the circumstances, your children may have some legal claim on your assets. In a community property state, your spouse has no legal right to inherit your property. Outside of these rules, it is not necessary to disinherit anyone – you simply do not leave them any portion of your estate.

The concept of disinheritance primarily applies to your children. No matter which state you live in, you can always disinherit your children, as long as you expressly state that this is the case in your will. It is not necessary to state why you are disinheriting, only that you are specifically excluding the named person from inheriting any assets. The worst situation is to not name the child in your will, in which case it could be claimed that you accidentally overlooked the child in your will – which entitles the child to some inheritance rights. However, the child will only have inheritance rights if he or she files a lawsuit that contests the contents of your will.

Summary

There are several types of beneficiaries, so you should be aware of the differences between them when deciding upon who will receive your assets after you die. There are also several clauses that can be inserted into your will that address certain issues that can impact beneficiaries, such as what happens when both spouses die at the same time. These clauses can be used to ensure that your assets are distributed to the beneficiaries you want, and in the intended amounts.

Chapter 3
Children Issues

Introduction

From an estate planning perspective, issues with children primarily involve minors, not children who have reached their adult years. This chapter deals extensively with minors, since there are few planning issues of concern once they become adults. The main issues are how to ensure that assets left to a minor will be handled responsibly in the event of the parents' untimely death, as well as ensuring that the minor will be properly cared for.

> **Tip:** Whenever you have an additional child, revise your estate plan to provide for it, to ensure that the new child receives what you feel is the appropriate percentage of your estate. Similarly, if a child dies, revise the estate plan to redirect your assets to your other children (or other beneficiaries).

Assigning Responsibility for Raising Your Child

Normally, when there are two parents – either biological or adoptive – the surviving parent is legally responsible for raising the child. What should you do to guard against a situation in which both parents die? Ideally, another person becomes the child's personal guardian. This person should be named in your will, and will become the personal guardian if approved by the applicable court following your death. The court may conclude that a different party should be the guardian if doing so will be in the best interests of the child, perhaps because your nominee has a criminal background or is an alcoholic. Naming a different person is rare, unless someone contests your choice of guardian.

The choice of guardian is obviously a major one, since it will have a significant impact on your child. First, the person should be willing to take on the task, and have the financial resources to do so. Also, be aware that the personal circumstances of a guardian can change over time, to the extent that the person may refuse to take on this substantial responsibility. To guard against that eventuality, consider naming a backup guardian who is willing to step in if the primary designee refuses to do so.

There may be cases in which you do not want the other parent to be your child's personal guardian. For example, the other parent might be an alcoholic, or is unstable. As a general rule, it is difficult to block the other parent from becoming the guardian, unless the other person can be proven to be unfit for parenting, or has legally abandoned the child. It can be quite difficult to prove that the other parent is unfit for parenting, unless there is a clear history of serious issues. Consequently, if you name someone else to be your child's guardian, be aware that this person might be in for a substantial legal battle over custody.

It is quite unlikely that anyone other than the other parent can gain custody of your child against the guardian preference stated in your will. For example, the child's aunt would be unlikely to gain custody.

Tip: Coordinate your choice of guardian with your spouse (or whoever else is jointly raising your child with you), to avoid assigning the guardianship to two different people in those rare cases in which both parents die at the same time.

If you do not think that the chosen guardian will do a good job of managing the money you are leaving for your child, you can appoint someone else to look after the money. This can result in a difficult relationship between the two parties, so be sure that they are willing to work together. A possible option is to leave assets to your spouse, who will manage them on behalf of your children; this approach should only be considered if your spouse is a prudent money manager. You might also want to assign a property manager if your children are adults, but still rather young. It is common for a property manager to oversee assets until your children reach a more mature age, such as 30 or 35.

A property manager is supposed to administer your assets in a manner that is in the best interests of your children, and to do so in a prudent manner. This means that funds should be directed toward the normal living expenses of the child, as well as to pay for educational and health requirements as they arise. When there are substantial assets involved, it is common for the property manager for pay for technical support, such as an investment counsellor and a tax advisor.

Tip: It is acceptable to appoint a couple to be guardians for your children. However, do so only if these people have similar parenting styles and are likely to remain married for an extended period of time. Anything else might be upsetting for your children.

Whomever your choice of guardian may be, it can be useful to write a letter and attach it to your will, explaining your reasoning. For example:

> I have nominated my second husband, Greg, to be the personal guardian of my son Nate from my first marriage. Greg has been an excellent parent for the last five years, living with us both and taking care of Nate. Nate's father left six years ago and has not been seen since, so Nate considers Greg to be his father. Nate and Greg have an excellent relationship, so I believe Greg would be the best possible choice to be Nate's personal guardian.

An attorney can provide assistance in the drafting of this letter, since it may be reviewed by a judge as part of a disputed custody proceeding.

Tip: Depending on state law, the biological parent may be the only legal one in cases where the parents are not married. See a local attorney for more information.

Property Management Options

There are several methods available for leaving property to your children. These options are noted in the following subsections.

Custodianship

Assets can be gifted to children under the terms of the Uniform Transfers to Minors Act (UTMA), where the property manager is referred to as the custodian. Under this approach, you state the property to be gifted to the minor, and who will be the custodian under the terms of the UTMA. The custodian can then manage the property for the benefit of the minor, acting prudently. The custodian must also keep records that can then be used to file tax returns on behalf of the minor. The custodian can be paid a reasonable amount in exchange for these services. Once the minor reaches the age specified in the UTMA, he or she receives the remaining amount of the property. A concern with this option is that the custodianship ends when the minor is legally an adult – which may still be quite young to be given responsibility for what may be a substantial estate.

Child's Trust

A child's trust is used to leave specific assets to a child. This means that you can create a separate child's trust for each child. A *trust* is a separate legal entity that owns assets, where a responsible party (a trustee) manages the assets.

A child's trust can be configured to operate in a variety of ways. The trustee can be given specific instructions to give the beneficiaries a certain amount of income yearly, or spend the money on their behalf. The trustee could also be given broad discretion to give the beneficiaries money as needs arise, such as for college tuition or medical expenses. Often, child's trusts are established to last until the designated child reaches a certain age, but they could also be extended well into adulthood in order to prevent spendthrift activity. It is also possible to initiate a child's trust when the person is already legally an adult, if you feel that the person will not be able to responsibly handle the gifted assets.

When a child's trust is established as part of a living trust[1], all property placed within the trust sidesteps probate[2]. Conversely, if the trust is established through your will, then it must first go through probate before the property can be placed within the trust.

---

[1] A *living trust* is a trust created during a person's lifetime where the trustee is given responsibility for managing that person's assets for the benefit of the eventual beneficiary. A living trust is designed to allow for the easy transfer of assets while avoiding the legal process of probate.

[2] *Probate* is a legal process that takes place after someone dies. It includes proving in court that a deceased person's will is valid, identifying the person's property, having the property appraised, paying debts and taxes, and distributing the remaining property as the will or the law directs. Attorney and court fees are paid from the estate property, which would otherwise go to the beneficiaries.

> **Note:** The provisions of a child's trust will never take effect if the child's age exceeds the provisions of the trust before you die. At that point, the trust arrangement is never triggered, and the child (now an adult) receives the property directly.

> **Tip:** A grandparent might elect to use a child's trust to leave assets to his or her grandchildren.

A child's trust formed under the provisions of the UTMA is relatively simple and inexpensive to operate. That being the case, it is more applicable when the value of the gifted assets is relatively low, or when you want it to be operated for a number of years past when the child is legally an adult (when annual trust operating costs are more likely to pile up). Also, assets in a child's trust are taxed at the child's individual tax rate, which tends to be relatively low.

EXAMPLE

Doris has three daughters. Abbie and Bonnie are prudent with their cash, while Charlize spends whatever she receives instantly. Based on their spending behaviors, Doris creates a living trust in which Abbie and Bonnie receive one-third of her estate immediately upon her demise, while Charlize's one-third share is parked in a child's trust. The trustee will dole out the contents of the trust to Charlize over a ten-year period, so that the funds are not squandered immediately.

Family Pot Trust

Under a family pot trust arrangement (and as the name implies), assets are left in a common pot for at least two children. The assets within this trust can be spent for any child covered by it. This means that the amounts spent do not have to be equally allocated to each child. This trust generally remains in operation until the youngest person covered by it is 18 years old, though an older age can be selected. The characteristics of a family pot trust are otherwise similar to those of a child's trust.

Property Guardian

The least-used option is a property guardian, who manages any portion of your child's assets that are not already being managed by a custodianship or trust. This is essentially a backstop for the other property management options, to ensure that all stray property not covered by the other options is still being properly managed. These guardians are subject to court oversight, which can result in expensive court filings – the cost of which comes out of the child's assets. It is useful to name a property guardian in your will; otherwise, the court will appoint someone who may not be as competent as the person you select.

Educational Investment Plans

It is possible to save for a child's education in a tax-advantaged manner. One option is the 529 plan, which is designed to pay for the educational expenses of a specific beneficiary who must be a family member. All income earned within a 529 plan is not taxed. However, contributions made into this plan are not tax deductible. The expenses that qualify for reimbursement from a 529 plan include tuition and fees, books, and supplies. If the named beneficiary does not use all of the funds in a 529 plan, you can name another family member as the replacement beneficiary.

Note: Taxes and penalties will apply if you ever withdraw cash from a 529 plan for noneducational purposes.

A 529 plan is controlled by local state law, and is managed by an investment company. While most states allow anyone to invest in their plans, some restrict these plans to residents. Another issue to research is the size of the investment fees charged, which can vary substantially by state.

Tip: Some states allow you to deduct your contributions to a 529 plan from your state income tax bill, which might convince you to use your state's 529 plan.

There are two types of 529 plans. One option is structured in a manner similar to a 401(k) plan, where you are expected to continue adding funds to the plan over an extended period of time, and expect to earn a return on your invested funds. Another option is the prepaid plan, where you pay the full amount of the expected educational costs in advance. A prepaid plan may be designed to lock in educational costs for certain state schools, or it may be used to pay for the educational costs of a private college. If the planned expenditures are not made by the student, then the remaining balance in the account can be shifted into a different plan, or you can assign the balance to a beneficiary.

There are several problems with 529 plans. One is the high fees charged by the plan administrators. Another concern is that the investment strategies used by the various plans differ widely, which can alter your expected return or risk profile beyond what you expect. Yet another concern is that the investment options within each plan tend to be quite limited, so you may be confined to an investment approach that you do not like.

Another educational investment option is the educational savings account. Contributions into these accounts are not tax deductible, but any earnings are not taxed, as long as withdrawals are made to pay for qualified educational expenses. Investments made into these accounts are not restricted, so you can use any investment strategy you want. However, the annual cap on contributions to these plans is severely restricted, and is not available at all to those with higher incomes. Consequently, educational savings accounts are of the most use to lower-income households that have limited cash available to invest. They might also be used by grandparents who want to make modest contributions to the educational costs of their grandchildren.

Children as Life Insurance Beneficiaries

If you are unable to set aside significant assets for your children, another option is to purchase term life insurance, which is the least expensive form of life insurance. If you die, then the insurer pays your children the amount of the policy (assuming that you designate them as the beneficiaries). However, if the children are still minors when you die, then the insurer cannot pay the funds directly to them. Instead, a property guardian will have to oversee the funds. A good way to avoid the disruption (and cost) associated with a property guardian is to name a custodian under the UTMA, using a form provided by the insurer. Another option is to use a child's trust or pot trust as part of a living trust to channel the insurance proceeds to your children, where the living trust or trustee is named as the policy beneficiary.

Children Conceived After Your Death

If a parent has his or her sperm or eggs (respectively) frozen, then it is possible for a pregnancy to be initiated after they have died – possibly years later. How this situation is to be handled varies widely by state. Generally, such a child is considered to have some rights to the estate of his or her parents, though the supporting conditions can differ by state government. For example, the following factors may need to be present:

- The parent who has died stated in writing that his or her genetic material could be used to subsequently conceive a child, and signed the document.
- Someone has been given control by the parent over the genetic material.
- Written notice was given to the parent's executor that such genetic material was available.
- The child was conceived within a certain period of time following the death of the parent.

A knowledgeable local attorney should be consulted before making inheritance decisions in this area.

Leaving Property to Other Children

There may be cases in which you want to leave assets to children who are not your own. There are several ways to do so. The easiest approach is to gift to the child's parent or guardian, with a request for that person to ensure that the asset is used to benefit the child. Of course, this requires a certain amount of trust in the reliability of the recipient. Another option is to create a child's trust for the assets, in which case you will also need to appoint a trustee. The latter approach is a common one when a grandparent wants to leave assets for a grandchild, and can rely on the parent to act as the trustee. The worst option is to simply state the gift of assets in your will, since the recipient (if still a minor at the time of your death) will be legally unable to receive it. Instead, the court must appoint a property guardian to oversee how the gift is used.

Summary

The essential issues regarding estate planning for your children are who will be responsible for raising them and how to designate a custodian who will oversee any assets left to them. Since the number of children you have may change over time, it makes sense to review and adjust these estate planning issues every few years.

Chapter 4
Essentials of Wills

Introduction

A will is a legal document in which is specified who receives your property when you die. It can also cover such issues as the appointment of a guardian for your children. A will is essential for the disposition of your estate, even though the property gifted through a will must first go through the expensive and time-consuming probate process. In this chapter, we discuss the need for a will, how it should be structured, types of wills, and several related issues.

The Need for a Will

A will is the core document within your overall estate planning process. In many cases where the disposition of assets is relatively simple, it is likely that you will initially need nothing more than a will – especially if you are mostly concerned with simply ensuring that your assets are distributed to the correct parties. Also, it is easier to amend a will than it is to amend a living trust, and you can use a will to appoint a guardian for your children. Other aspects of estate planning are more expensive, so you might want to wait until later in life, when more funds are (presumably) available to craft a more comprehensive estate planning strategy.

You might be tempted to park all assets in a trust, in order to avoid probate. However, this is not always possible for some assets – especially automobiles. Insurers tend not to react favorably to a request to insure a vehicle that is owned by a trust. For these types of assets, the only real option is to gift them through your will. Another case in which a will is useful is when you unexpectedly acquire property towards the end of your life, such as an inheritance, and do not have time to adjust your trust documents to account for it. Or, you may be about to receive property from someone else that is currently stuck in the probate process, but which cannot yet be included in your living trust because you do not yet own it. As a backstop, the presence of a will ensures that this additional property will be gifted to your residuary beneficiary, who will receive all remaining property not gifted elsewhere in your estate plan.

> **Note:** Property must be specifically added to a living trust before it will be subject to the provisions of the trust. This means that quite a large number of assets need to be covered by default through your will.

Another good reason to have a will is so that you can name the executor for your estate. The *executor* is legally empowered to oversee the distribution of the assets within your estate.

> **Tip:** It is more efficient to have the same person be your executor and the trustee of your living trust.

A final reason to have a will is that some states only require a modest probate process – or none at all – when your estate is quite small. In this case, there is no reason to adopt more complex probate avoidance methods – just a will may be all you need.

Requirements for a Will

There are comparatively few requirements for the creation of a will. The following conditions must be present for a will to be considered valid:

- You must be at least 18 years old.
- You must be of sound mind.
- You must appoint an executor.
- The will must be typewritten, dated, and signed in front of two adults who are not beneficiaries. The witnesses must also sign the document.

The witnesses do not have to read the will; they must only know that it is a will you are signing. It is not necessary for the will to be notarized, nor do you have to file it with any government department.

A will is valid even if you prepare it while residing in another country, as long as you follow the requirements just stated and have a legal stateside residence. If you do not have a legal stateside residence, then use the rules of the state in which you are legally able to vote.

> **Note:** A will signed in one state is still valid if you then move to another state. However, it is advisable to issue a new will when you permanently switch to a new state, especially when you are moving from a community property state to a common law state, or vice versa.

Types of Wills

There are multiple types of wills, of which the most common is the *formal will*. This is a properly typed, signed, and witnessed document that assigns assets to beneficiaries, and may also appoint an executor, as well as a guardian for any minors. This will can be used in a backup role when other estate planning tools, such as a living trust, are being used to distribute assets. A backup will is essentially intended to deal with any issues not covered elsewhere in your estate plan.

It is also possible to create an *electronic will*. This document is created, signed, and stored online. To be legally valid, witnesses still need to sign it. This approach is not valid in most states, so review the issue with a local attorney before creating an electronic will. There are still issues with electronic wills, such as how to verify the identity of the parties involved, as well as what constitutes a signature, so it is best to use a traditional (printed) will.

A *statutory will* is a standardized form in which you check a few boxes and fill in a few blanks – and presto, you have a will. This approach is certainly inexpensive and requires minimal time to complete. However, these formats are also quite limited and cannot be altered, and so only apply to a small subset of the population. They are also only considered valid within a few states. A better approach is to develop a will that has been customized to your specific circumstances.

A *joint will* is a single document that has been created by two people (usually a married pair). Under this format, each person leaves all assets to the other person, after which the will describes how the assets will be apportioned after both people have died. This arrangement does not allow the surviving person to make alternative decisions about how the remaining property will be gifted. This approach is generally not recommended, since the circumstances of the surviving person may subsequently change considerably, calling for a different apportionment of assets to beneficiaries.

A *pour-over will* directs that the assets subjected to it be transferred into a trust. The trust document then describes how the assets will be distributed to beneficiaries. These wills are not recommended, because they do not avoid probate – which delays the distribution of assets. Instead, use other estate planning tools to keep the bulk of your assets out of probate, and then use a backup will to distribute any remaining assets.

A handwritten will is written entirely by the person leaving assets, who must also sign and date it. This type of will does not have to be witnessed. However, due to the lack of a witnessing requirement, these wills are not valid in many states, and will be challenged in others on the grounds that the will could have been forged. Consequently, it makes more sense to have a formal will typed up and properly witnessed.

A video will is not a valid will. However, such a production, where the individual states who receives property and why, can be used as evidence in court to support a contested will. This approach is especially useful when it appears likely that someone might contest your will on the grounds that you are of unsound mind.

Explanatory Documentation

In addition to a will, it can be useful to leave a letter to be attached to your will, describing the reasons why you left property to certain beneficiaries. This letter should state that it is separate from your will, and is only intended to provide your reasoning for the allocations contained within the will. For example, it might explain why you left a particular painting to a niece, or why a favorite property has been gifted to a distant relative. The usual reasons for unusual allocations are that one person is more needy than the other heirs and so is given more assets, or that one person has already received an excessive amount of cash, and so will be left fewer assets in the will.

It can also be useful to give your reasons for appointing a particular person to the post of executor. A common approach is to have the eldest person be the executor, so it can be useful to explain why the position is being given to someone else (perhaps because he or she is an accountant).

An explanatory letter is also a good place in which to express your appreciation for those in your life, such as the years of support by a care-giver. Conversely, it makes little sense to lambast someone, especially since that person could sue your estate for libel. In general, be generous in making positive comments, and try to avoid negative ones.

This letter has absolutely no legal status, but might be useful in soothing the feelings of anyone whose feelings might be hurt by the contents of your will.

Property Not Transferred Through a Will

As a general rule, property that is already set to be transferred through an estate planning tool designed to avoid probate cannot also be transferred through your will. For example, if you place property in a living trust, then that property will be gifted to the beneficiaries designated in the living trust, irrespective of what is stated in your will. Similarly, if you have joint tenancy property (such as your house), then your share of the property goes to the surviving joint tenants, even if you state otherwise in your will. As a third example, the formally-stated beneficiaries of your life insurance policy will receive the policy payout upon your death, even if the terms of your will contradict this arrangement.

Special Considerations

A special consideration is what to do in the event of a divorce. While some states automatically remove will provisions that leave assets to your ex-spouse, it is best to issue a revised will that reallocates assets away from this person. Another situation calling for a revised will is when you subsequently get married or have children. Gifts to these additional parties should be explicitly stated in the will, so that they are not accidentally excluded from your estate.

The Success of Challenges to Your Will

Successful challenges to a will make for good television, but are actually quite rare in the real world. A will can only be successfully challenged under unusual circumstances. These challenges usually question whether you were of sound mind, or under duress, or under some degree of undue influence when you made the will. The default assumption by any court is that you were of sound mind and not being adversely influenced, so the challenger must prove otherwise in court.

In cases where you think someone might challenge your will, see an attorney about installing safeguards. The attorney might want to be present when you sign your will, in order to later attest in court to the soundness of your mind at that time.

Summary

It is best to have an attorney construct a formal will on your behalf. Doing so improves the likelihood that the will addresses all issues relevant to your situation. This approach also minimizes the risk of having someone challenge the will at a later date. You should revise your will at regular intervals, such as once every five years, in order to incorporate any changes to your personal circumstances and the people you want to designate as beneficiaries.

Chapter 5
Probate Issues

Introduction

Probate is a time-consuming and potentially expensive bottleneck that must be addressed before your estate can distribute assets to your designated beneficiaries. In this chapter, we discuss the probate concept, how to avoid it, and the rare cases in which it can be useful.

What is Probate?

Probate is the legal process of distributing a decedent's[3] assets. When someone dies, he or she usually leaves behind assets to distribute and debts to pay. Even among those who have a will detailing who gets the house, furniture, and securities, the assets must still go through probate. When an estate goes through probate, the executor files paperwork in probate court to start the process. The executor must first prove to the court the validity of the person's property and beneficiaries. The court then decides whether to sell the assets to pay debts and taxes before distributing assets to the beneficiaries of the decedent's estate. During this process, the executor also manages the assets. An extended probate process reduces the amount of money left over for beneficiaries, because the decedent's estate is required to pay court and attorney fees. These attorney fees can be considerable, since many executors hire an attorney to oversee the probate process on behalf of the estate. The work of this attorney is primarily administrative, involving the completion of a number of court forms and ensuring that filings are made prior to the court's deadlines. The attorney's fees can pile up, because the probate process can take well over a year to complete.

The implication throughout this book is that the probate process is to be avoided, since it consumes a great deal of time during which assets cannot be distributed to beneficiaries, and because it can be expensive. However, it also reduces the amount of fraud that might otherwise arise, where someone might attempt to steal the decedent's assets. Probate also provides a structured process for resolving any claims that may be brought against the estate. That being said, the settlement of most estates is relatively simple, involving distributions to only a small number of family members. There also tend to be few creditor claims on a decedent's estate. Consequently, the probate process can be considered inefficient and not necessary for most estates.

When a decedent did not create a will, or if the will was improperly constructed and no other estate planning methods were used, then the decedent's estate must go through this probate process.

---

[3] A *decedent* is a person who is no longer living.

When to Use Probate

There are a few cases in which it can make sense to run an estate through probate; in particular, when the estate has a large number of significant liabilities. We are not referring to standard liabilities, such as mortgage payments and utilities, but rather to large personal loans. In this situation, having the probate process being handled within the formal environment of a court makes it easier to resolve disputes, since the court has procedures to deal with these situations. In this environment, creditor claims can be settled relatively quickly, and certainly quicker than is the case when a creditor files a lawsuit against the estate. Within the probate structure, creditors must file a claim with the court within a certain number of months of being notified of the probate proceeding, or else their claim will be ignored.

Probate is also useful in cases where you suspect that someone might contest your estate plan via a lawsuit. Under probate rules, the burden is on the challenger to prove that the estate plan should be voided, which is not easy to prove. In addition, probate only allows the challenger a relatively short period of time in which to prove his or her case.

A third reason to use probate is to avoid the risk of having to pay unexpected creditor claims. When probate is used, creditors are notified that the estate is in probate, and have a limited amount of time in which to file claims. If the creditors do not file claims, then they have no further recourse. If the beneficiaries believe that there may be substantial and possibly undocumented claims against the estate, they may want to force the estate into probate in order to eliminate the risk of having additional claims come to light at a later date.

> **Note:** When there is no probate, the party responsible for paying any debts and taxes associated with the estate is the beneficiary. If there are several beneficiaries, then the executor will likely have to determine the responsibility.

If no one pays the debts and taxes associated with an estate, then there is no time limit on creditor claims – so the beneficiaries of the estate could be liable for a very long time.

> **Tip:** A good way to settle the debts and taxes associated with an estate is to set aside a cash reserve for this purpose. Any residual funds in this reserve are eventually distributed to the beneficiaries, but not until the executor is sure that all obligations of the estate have been settled.

The Cost of Probate

There are several types of costs that can be charged against a decedent's estate as part of the probate process. As just noted, the attorney who administers the paperwork associated with the probate process will charge hourly fees throughout the process. In most states, it is essential to hire an attorney for this work. In addition, the executor who oversees the estate is also entitled to charge fees to the estate. However, the executor is frequently also a beneficiary of the estate, and so does not benefit from charging any fees. The probate court will also charge fees, including a filing fee and fees for the production of certified court documents.

The end result of these costs is that a decedent's estate may be significantly shrunken in size by the time a distribution is finally made to the beneficiaries. To keep this from happening, it makes a great deal of sense to keep your most valuable assets out of the probate process entirely. By doing so, the small residual asset balance may fall below the threshold set by the applicable state government, thereby allowing the executor to skip probate entirely for all assets.

Avoiding Probate

There are a variety of techniques available for avoiding probate. We summarize these options in the following table, which describes each option and then presents the advantages and disadvantages associated with it.

Probate Avoidance Techniques

Avoidance Technique	Advantages	Disadvantages
Joint tenancy	Simple to create and effective	Each party can sell their interest
Life insurance	Good way to provide beneficiaries with the cash to pay estate taxes	The cost of the insurance may exceed the benefits from its use
Living trust	Gives you control over assets while you live	Can be relatively costly to establish
Minimum state-level probate avoidance thresholds	Can be a good way to keep residual assets out of probate	The probate avoidance threshold varies by state
Name a beneficiary to your pension plan	Simple to create and effective	Transfers may be capped or prohibited by the pension plan
Pay-on-death bank accounts	Simple to create and effective	Only applies to bank accounts
Tenancy by the entirety	Simple to create and effective	Only available in some states
Transfer-on-death car registration	Simple to create and effective	Only applies in a minority of states
Transfer-on-death real estate deeds	Moderately easy to create and effective	Not available in all states
Transfer-on-death securities registration	Simple to create and effective	Not available in all states

Note: A creditor that is concerned about being paid can file a court action that will require probate proceedings to take place – which makes it helpful to ensure that all creditor claims are promptly settled.

There are cases in which the distribution of assets can be conducted on an informal basis. This is most common when someone has few assets, none of which have formal title documents associated with them. For example, a grandfather who lives alone sells his house and car, and moves into a retirement home. At the time of his death, he has minimal furniture, and his checking account is held jointly with his children. In this case, the children can agree upon who takes his furniture, and how to distribute the cash remaining in the checking account. These actions effectively settle his estate. This approach is not possible when the decedent has title to a house or other major assets.

Note: If the beneficiaries of an estate want to informally avoid probate, then all of them need to agree about how the assets of the estate are to be settled. Otherwise, anyone who does not like the proposed distribution can file a court action that will require probate proceedings.

Summary

Probate is a lengthy and potentially costly process for settling a decedent's estate, and so should be avoided where possible. We discuss one of the main tools for probate avoidance – living trusts – in the next chapter.

Chapter 6
Essentials of Living Trusts

Introduction

One of the best ways to transfer property without probate is the *living trust*, which is a legal document that lets you distribute your possessions to beneficiaries after you die. This trust owns the property you put into it, while still allowing you to maintain control. You can put most types of assets into a living trust, such as real estate, securities, and your bank accounts. It is similar to a will, but unlike a will, the property held within it avoids probate. We cover many aspects of living trusts in the following pages.

> **Terms:** A *trust* is established to provide protection to a set of assets and ensure that those assets are distributed correctly. The person who sets up a living trust is the *grantor*. The assets transferred into a trust are the *trust property*. Anyone who has control over the trust is called the *trustee*. Those who receive assets from the trust property after the grantor dies are *beneficiaries*.

Advantages of a Living Trust

There are several advantages to using a living trust, of which the most obvious is that it avoids the probate process. This sidesteps the substantial cost of probate, as well as the extended time period during which probate runs before assets can be distributed to beneficiaries. A further advantage is that the terms of living trusts are not normally made public when you die, which is not the case in the probate process. In addition, you can alter a revocable living trust at any time while you are still alive, and can do whatever you want with the property while you are living, including selling it. And yet another advantage is that there is no need to maintain separate tax records or acquire a taxpayer identification number for the trust; instead, all transactions involving the trust are included in your personal income tax return.

EXAMPLE

Henry owns an extensive antique car collection, which he wants to leave to his equally car-obsessed son, Geoffrey. Henry wants to maintain total control over the collection until he dies, including the right to sell any cars he wants (especially if the resulting cash can be used to acquire that sweet Bugatti Royale he has always wanted). He does not want this valuable collection to be subject to the public airing out associated with the probate process. Further, he sees no reason for his estate to spend a large amount of cash on probate fees when he just wants to turn the collection over to his son.

Accordingly, Henry sets up a living trust, with the car collection as its sole assets. He is the trustee, with absolute power to control the trust property. Geoffrey is both the successor trustee and the sole beneficiary. When Henry dies, Geoffrey, acting as the successor trustee, turns all trust assets over to himself, as the beneficiary. The trust then ceases to exist.

As a point of clarification (and as a clear advantage of a living trust), the IRS considers living trust assets to be part of your other assets, so there is no need to file a separate tax return for it, or maintain separate accounting records. Also, there is no tax benefit or loss associated with putting assets into a living trust.

As a further point of clarification, there is no tax advantage to using a living trust. It does not save estate taxes. The main point behind its use is to avoid the probate process.

When to Use a Living Trust (or Not)

There are several situations in which it makes more sense to set up a living trust, and other situations in which alternative choices will be better for you. First, an older and more infirm person is in a better position to use a living trust. A younger and healthier person can probably get by with a will that is updated regularly, since there is little likelihood of death at this point. Second, there are other options for avoiding probate that might work for you, such as the use of transfer-on-death accounts or joint tenancy arrangements. If doing so addresses the transfer of most of your assets, then that may be sufficient. Third, a living trust has no method for expeditiously settling creditor debts, so it can make sense to let the estate run through probate instead, where there is a process for creditors to file claims, after which all further claims are cut off. Fourth, a living trust works best when your assets are substantial; if that is not the case, probate fees may be minimal. Finally, a living trust is more workable when a trustworthy person will be the successor trustee. If that is not the case, you may need to use probate instead. In probate, the court will appoint a professional to oversee the distribution of your estate.

How Does a Living Trust Work?

A living trust is established through the filing of paperwork, in which you name yourself as the trustee (to manage the assets during your life), as well as a successor trustee who distributes the assets after your death. You also list the beneficiaries, who eventually receive the assets. This document transfers the named assets into the trust. That's it; the trust document does not have to be especially long, and is not complex. Further, you can change it at any time.

Couples commonly use a living will for the property owned by both of them. This approach is frequently used to pass property to their children. Or, each of the spouses might choose to create a separate living trust, if their property holdings are mostly separate. When one spouse dies, the trust is expanded into two trusts, where one trust contains the property of the spouse who has died (including that spouse's half ownership of all shared property in the trust), while the other trust contains the property of the remaining (living) spouse. It is quite possible that the sole beneficiary of the deceased spouse's trust assets is the surviving spouse, though other beneficiaries might also have been named.

If you become mentally unfit to manage the estate, then the successor trustee takes over and manages it on your behalf for the remainder of your life.

Once you die, the terms of the trust can no longer be altered. At that point, the successor trustee can transfer assets to the designated beneficiaries right away, with no need to enter the probate process. Once all assets have been distributed, the trust is eliminated.

> **Tip:** If you have significant debts, consider stating in the living trust which assets should be liquidated in order to pay for them. This can impact which assets will be left over to gift to beneficiaries.

> **Note:** A living trust can be named as the beneficiary of your life insurance policy. The trust is then used to name the beneficiaries of the life insurance proceeds. The result is that the policy proceeds avoid probate, going straight to the beneficiaries named in your living trust.

Living Trust Decisions

When creating a living trust, there are several decisions to be made. A key decision is how many assets to include in it. You have other vehicles by which assets can avoid probate; if so, by all means use them. All remaining large-dollar assets, and especially anything involving ownership documents, should be included in the living trust.

EXAMPLE

Christopher and Jessica Hood own a home together, held in joint tenancy, that has equity in it of $800,000. They also own a securities portfolio worth $420,000, as well as a variety of personal possessions. They have each decided to leave their half of all assets to the surviving spouse. Since the home is already held in joint tenancy, the surviving spouse will become the 100% owner without having to go through probate. They decide to create a living trust for the remaining assets.

> **Tip:** There is no need to contact your insurer or lender about having placed your home in a living trust. You remain the owner of the home for the remainder of your life, so do not confuse the issue with third parties.

Another decision is who to appoint as the trustee. The initial trustee will probably be you – the person who set it up, and the person whose assets are being controlled by the trust. Or, if you are married, you and your spouse will typically serve as co-trustees. It is also possible to name a third party as the trustee, perhaps because you are too infirm to manage the assets yourself. If so, you should set up strict controls over the powers of the trustee. Also, separate trust records will need to be maintained when a third party is the trustee, and a separate tax return will need to be filed.

A key decision is who will be the successor trustee. This person oversees the trust after you have died, with the primary goal of distributing assets to the beneficiaries. The successor trustee also pays any remaining debts and taxes from the estate assets. The successor trustee takes on a fair amount of responsibility, since this person has to obtain copies of your death certificate, and presents them, along with a copy of the living trust, to any institutions exercising control over your assets. For example, a successor trustee would present these documents to your bank in order to take control of your checking and savings accounts. This position is frequently assigned to one of the main beneficiaries, but name someone else if this person has trouble dealing with picayune paperwork issues. Or, it is acceptable to name several people as co-trustees, but only do so if you think they will be able to get along in their trustee roles. Yet another possibility is to name a bank as your successor trustee, but be aware that this entity will charge fees for its services – which may be substantial.

Tip: It is more efficient to have your successor trustee also serve as your executor, so name the successor trustee as the executor in your will.

In addition, the successor trustee prepares all documents that transfer control of your assets to designated beneficiaries. For example, in order to transfer real estate to beneficiaries, the trustee would write a declaration stating that the successor trustee has taken over, due to the death of the original trustee, and a deed showing the beneficiaries as the new owners, and presents them to the appropriate land records office. The successor trustee also oversees the distribution of all other assets remaining in the trust, such as furniture, books, and jewelry, to the designated beneficiaries.

The successor trustee also serves a notification role, which is to tell all trust beneficiaries when the grantor has died, and how to contact the trustee. It may also be necessary to provide each beneficiary with a copy of the trust, depending on state law. It makes no sense not to provide beneficiaries with this information, since they might otherwise suspect that the trustee is withholding or misallocating assets, and may then initiate lawsuits.

Tip: Consider naming a backup to the successor trustee, in case your primary choice cannot serve in the role, perhaps due to infirmity or death.

A difficult issue is who to make responsible for deciding whether the original trustee has become incapacitated. This can be stated as requiring one or more doctor opinions, but can also be assigned to a friend or family member. If several people are given responsibility to make the decision, then the trust document should clarify how to settle differences amongst the group in making the decision.

A further decision is who shall be listed as beneficiaries of the trust. It is perfectly acceptable to list different proportions of trust assets to different beneficiaries. For example, you could leave 20% of the property to two of your children and the remaining 60% to the third child, on the grounds that the third child is disabled and so needs more monetary support. Or, you might leave some assets (such as a car) to one beneficiary, and your house to someone else. Or, in the common case where you have entered into a shared living trust with your spouse, each of you can specify beneficiaries for your shares of the assets. For example, you may have children from a prior marriage, in which case you want to leave a portion of your assets to them.

EXAMPLE

David and Anna have been married for 40 years, and decide to create a shared living trust. They have two children, Ben and Carrie. Each of them leaves the vast majority of their assets to the other. In addition, Ben leaves $50,000 to his favorite bowling education charity, while Carrie leaves $75,000 to her favorite women's rights charity. They both name Ben and Carrie as their alternate beneficiaries.

Creating the Trust Document

A trust document can certainly be prepared by an attorney who specializes in this activity, or you can do it yourself, usually with the aid of a how-to book or software. Whichever path you choose, be sure to include the following topics in the document:

- *Terms*. Define every legal term used in the document, to avoid any confusion about what the terms mean.
- *Named parties*. It must name the trustee, successor trustee, and beneficiaries.
- *Property*. It must identify all property that will be included in the trust. This property is itemized on schedules attached to the trust document.
- *Notarized signature*. Sign the trust document in front of a notary public. There is no need for additional witnesses.

Once the trust document has been created, title to the named property must be transferred to the trustee. For example, if the trustee's name is John Smith, then the title document for a vacation property listed as part of the living trust might state the trustee's name as "John Smith, Trustee for the John Smith Living Trust". This activity is not required for possessions that have no title documents associated with them, such as jewelry and paintings; instead, just list them on the property schedule attached to the trust document. Examples of property that *do* have title documents associated with them are bank accounts, investment accounts, mutual funds, real estate, safe deposit boxes, planes, and vehicles.

Note: In rare cases, state law requires that title to property be transferred to the name of the trust itself, rather than the name of the trustee.

Note: No gift tax liability is created by shifting property into a living trust, because the trust can be revoked at any time prior to your death.

Some government entities require you to use a special form to officially record the transfer of property into a living trust.

Updating the Trust Document

Over time, it is likely that you will acquire or dispose of assets. If so, update the living trust to reflect these changes. If you add property to the trust, then include it in the supporting schedule and make sure that the title to it is in the original trustee's name. If you sell property from the trust, remove it from the supporting schedule. It may also be necessary to change beneficiaries, perhaps because someone has died, married, or had children. Or, you may need to switch to a different successor trustee.

> **Tip:** Make a note in your calendar to review the terms of your living trust on a regular basis, and have an attorney make changes to the document as needed.

Many changes can be made to the trust document by including them in an amendment that is appended to the trust document, signed, and notarized. However, if the changes you want to make are substantial, it can make sense to clarify matters by replacing the trust document with a new one. This represents a continuation of the trust, which has the advantage of not requiring you to create new title documents for property covered by the trust. This is a good place in which to obtain the services of a knowledgeable attorney.

If you have entered into a living trust arrangement with a spouse, then the other person will have to agree to any subsequent changes made to the document. If that spouse dies, then his or her share of the trust is now considered irrevocable, at which point the successor trustee will distribute that person's share of the property in the trust. The surviving spouse now has sole control over his or her own share of the trust.

> **Note:** A living trust is valid in any state, so you do not need to revise it if you move to a different state.

If you choose to revoke your living trust, then do so in a signed document. If you have created a shared trust with a spouse, then either spouse (not both) can revoke it; doing so returns both spouses to their former ownership arrangement for the pertinent assets.

Summary

A living trust is commonly used to circumvent probate requirements, thereby eliminating probate costs and the extended time period during which estate assets are tied up in probate. This approach is highly recommended when you have substantial assets, though there are some circumstances in which it makes less sense to set up a living trust.

Chapter 7
Types of Tenancy

Introduction

This chapter explores the nature of joint tenancy, as well as tenancy by the entirety. These are useful conceptual tools for keeping some assets away from the probate process.

Essentials of Joint Tenancy

Joint tenancy refers to a legal arrangement in which two or more parties own a property together, with each person having equal rights and obligations. There are two ways to place property in a joint tenancy; either the joint tenants acquire the property and take title in joint tenancy, or someone who already owns property transfers the associated title into a joint tenancy with other parties. Joint tenancy is usually indicated on a legal document by placing the words "in joint tenancy" in the ownership document. A variation required in some states is to use the words "joint tenants with right of survivorship". The exact requirements for setting up a joint tenancy will vary somewhat by state.

Joint tenancies are most commonly associated with the ownership of real estate, but can be applied to any assets, such as art collections or valuable furniture. This merely requires that the co-owners declare in a document (preferably notarized) that you own the designated property as joint tenants.

EXAMPLE

Emily and Davis have accumulated an impressive collection of Southeast Asian artwork during their 30 years together. They mutually agree that the survivor should receive all of this artwork when the other one dies, and they want to avoid probate. Accordingly, they draw up a joint ownership document, in which they declare that all works of art listed in it are the property of their joint tenancy.

A joint tenancy may be created by married and un-married couples, as well as friends, relatives, and business associates.

A joint tenancy relationship creates a right of survivorship, so if one owner dies, that person's interest in the property is shifted directly to the surviving parties without having to go through the probate process.

EXAMPLE

Alice and Bert own their house and a securities account with a national brokerage in joint tenancy. When Alice dies, her one-half ownership of the house and securities account automatically transfers to Bert, who is now the 100% owner of both assets without having to go through the probate process.

Under this arrangement, the joint owners have an equal share of all profits and losses generated by their property. If the ownership document specifies different ownership levels among the owners, then (in most states) the arrangement is not considered a joint tenancy. Instead, the arrangement is considered to be a tenancy in common.

In short, in a joint tenancy arrangement, leaving property to anyone other than the other joint tenants is not allowed. For example, if you were to leave such property to a third party in your will, this would have no legal effect.

> **Tip:** If you decide to leave your interest in a joint tenancy asset to a third party, you can terminate the joint tenancy arrangement during your lifetime, shift the property over to a tenancy in common, and then assign the property to a different party.

There can be a few issues with a joint tenancy arrangement. First, all debts associated with the property are the equal responsibility of all owners. Second, none of the owners can sell the property without first obtaining the consent of all other partners. Third, joint tenancy gives all rights to the survivor, so even if the decedent wanted to pass the value of the property to his or her heirs, there is no legal obligation for the survivor to honor that request. In short, you should be aware of the associated issues before entering into a joint tenancy arrangement.

It is unlikely – but still possible – that you and your other joint tenants will all die at the same time. An option for dealing with this scenario is to name a beneficiary in your will who will inherit your share of the property. If you do not name such a person, your ownership interest will still pass to the residuary beneficiary.

> **Tip:** If you live in a community property state, spouses routinely hold their community property in joint tenancy with each other, in order to sidestep probate. In this situation, write a document stating that the joint tenancy property remains community property. Otherwise, title companies are prone to deny transfers of real estate.

In some states, a married couple can enter into a community property agreement, where they declare their property to be community property, thereby leaving it to the survivor without having to deal with probate. These agreements need to be witnessed or notarized, and may need to be filed in the county where their real estate is located.

Joint Tenancy Bank Accounts

When a couple is already pooling its cash reserves in a checking or savings bank account, it can make sense to designate the account as being a joint tenancy arrangement. This approach can be extended further, to include certificates of deposit. This is a common arrangement, so banks typically have forms already available to designate these accounts as such. Once one of the partners dies, the other person immediately gains ownership of all the cash in the applicable account.

> **Tip:** If you are concerned about having your spouse make large withdrawals from a joint tenancy account, ask if the bank will set up the account to require two signatures on all check payments from the account.

A concern with joint tenancy accounts is when you are planning to give the cash in the account to someone other than your spouse. Doing so gives that person immediate access to the cash in the account right now, which could lead to unexplained withdrawals. A good way to avoid this problem is to set up a pay-on-death account with the bank, which also avoids probate.

> **Note:** You are not creating a taxable gift if you create a joint bank account that names a third party as a co-owner of the account. However, there *is* a taxable gift if this other person takes money out of the account during your lifetime.

Joint Tenancy Safe Deposit Boxes

It may seem prudent to set up joint tenancy for the contents of a safe deposit box. This box typically contains your will, investment information, and jewelry. Depending on the situation, it can make sense to specify in the bank documents whether the joint owners of the box contents actually share ownership of those contents. For example, you might want to retain sole control over any jewelry stored in the box. In this case, the joint tenancy is really for access to the box, not its contents.

> **Tip:** Itemize who will receive the contents of your safe deposit box in your will or living trust document.

A particular concern with safe deposit boxes is whether they will be sealed by the bank when it is notified of the owner's death. This is most likely to occur in states that impose an estate tax. In this situation, the contents of the box will not be available until a representative of the state government has inventoried the box. For this reason, it may not make sense to store your will or living trust document in the box.

Essentials of Tenancy by the Entirety

Tenancy by the entirety refers to a form of shared property ownership that is reserved for the sole use of married couples. Under this arrangement, spouses can jointly own property as a single legal entity, which means that each spouse has an equal and undivided interest in the property. This form of ownership creates a right of survivorship, so that the surviving spouse automatically receives full title to the property without having to go through the probate process. This approach is only used in states that specifically allow it.

The terms of property use for a tenancy by the entirety are essentially the same as is found for a joint tenancy. The main difference is that it is only available to married couples.

Advantages of Joint Tenancies

There are several advantages associated with a joint tenancy arrangement. First, it is a good option for a married couple that wants to ensure that the surviving spouse gains ownership of the property when one of them dies. Second, making a property purchase in joint tenancy ensures that targeted property will transfer directly to the survivor, avoiding probate.

> **Tip:** If you have engaged in no estate planning and it is likely that you will die soon, a good option is to use a joint tenancy arrangement to avoid probate for targeted assets.

EXAMPLE

Eddie is already older than anyone in his family tree. He lives in a home on a pleasant tree-lined street in a town in central New York, and wants to leave it to his favorite son, Frank. He also wants to avoid probate, but without too much paperwork. A good choice is to transfer his ownership of the home into a joint tenancy with Frank. Doing so requires minimal paperwork. Also, Frank will benefit from the stepped-up basis of the home, once he inherits it.

Disadvantages of Joint Tenancies

There are a few issues with the joint tenancy concept. First, any joint tenant can terminate the arrangement while they are still alive, even without the consent of the other parties. This can greatly interfere with your estate planning, especially in regard to avoiding probate. This can be a major concern when you are contemplating transferring property into a joint tenancy, and then have a falling out with the other joint tenant. This person could end the joint tenancy and be left with a half-share of what had been your property.

EXAMPLE

Tom transfers his vacation home into a joint tenancy with his grand-niece Alice. Shortly afterwards, the two have a bitter fight over what to do with the property, and Alice ends the joint tenancy. She now has a 50% interest in the vacation home as a tenant in common, and petitions a court to order a sale of the property, so that she can extract her share in the form of cash.

To avoid the situation outlined in the preceding example, it can make more sense to transfer property through a living trust; in this case, you can maintain control over the property throughout your life, and alter the beneficiaries as much as you want.

Another concern with a joint tenancy is when one of the parties to the arrangement has substantial debts. Though creditors cannot access the interests of the other joint tenants in a property, they *can* convince a court to sell the entire property, so that they can be repaid. This situation only arises when the deceased party has used his or her interest in the property as collateral for a loan, or when the creditor was already taking steps to collect on a legal judgment when the party died. In short, entering into a joint tenancy with a highly indebted person can result in the property being sold out from under you in order to pay that person's debts.

A final concern is when one of the parties to a joint tenancy becomes so incapacitated that he or she cannot make decisions regarding the underlying property. A good mitigating action is to give a trusted person a power of attorney in regard to the use of the property, so that a sale transaction can proceed.

Tenancy Tax Issues

Before deciding whether to use joint tenancy or tenancy by the entirety, there are a few tax issues to be aware of. First, if the joint tenants are married, then half of the market value of the property as of the date of death of the first spouse is included in that person's taxable estate for federal tax purposes. This is the case even if one spouse paid disproportionately more to acquire the property.

EXAMPLE

Thelma and Louis are married and live in Moab, Utah. They acquired real estate 10 years ago as a tenancy by the entirety. Louis paid for the down payment on the property from his savings account, while all subsequent mortgage payments were roughly shared between them. Louis then dies by driving his car off a cliff. According to the IRS, half of the market value of the property is included in Louis's taxable estate, even though he contributed a larger amount of cash to the property.

This is not the case when the couple entering into a joint tenancy is not married. In this situation, the value of each person's interest is based on that person's contributions to the property. For example, if one person has paid the down payment on a property, plus all subsequent mortgage payments, then the full market value of the property becomes part of her estate upon her death.

Tip: If you are not married and own property in a joint tenancy arrangement, then keep excellent records concerning who paid for the property, to ensure that the value of the estate is correctly apportioned upon your death.

No gift taxes are incurred when property is transferred by either spouse into a joint tenancy arrangement, or when gifts are made by one spouse to the other. However, a gift tax situation can arise when the parties are not married; in this case, when the parties do not pay an equal amount for a property, the party paying more has essentially gifted the excess amount to the other party.

EXAMPLE

Diana transfers her $800,000 home to a joint tenancy arrangement with her son Evan in order to avoid the probate process. By doing so, she has made a $400,000 gift (one-half of the home's value) to her son, which is subject to the federal gift tax (less an annual exemption).

Under federal estate tax law, the party inheriting joint tenancy property is awarded a stepped-up basis in the value of the property, which is used as the basis for calculating any gains on the property when it is eventually sold. This can be a massive benefit for the beneficiary, if the market value of the property has risen substantially.

EXAMPLE

Dianne acquired her home for $275,000. She dies and leaves the home to her daughter, Margaret. On the day of Dianne's death, the market value of her home is $790,000. When Margaret inherits the house, her tax basis in it is stepped up to the $790,000 value. Thus, if she were to sell the property for that amount, she would report no taxable gain.

How does this step-up concept apply to a joint tenancy arrangement? In this case, the survivor is awarded a stepped-up basis for that half-portion of the property owned by the deceased party. The other half already owned by the survivor retains its original tax basis.

EXAMPLE

Arnold and Melissa purchase a home for $600,000 and structure it as a joint tenancy. When Arnold dies, the property has a market value of $1,000,000. The basis of Arnold's half-share of the home is stepped up to $500,000, while the basis of Melissa's share remains at $300,000 – which is her share of the original purchase price. In aggregate, this means that Melissa's revised total basis in her home is now $800,000.

> **Note:** Depending on local rules, the value of real estate may be reassessed whenever there is a change of ownership – usually resulting in a notable increase in property taxes. Usually, creating a joint tenancy does not constitute a change of ownership, unless the original owner is not one of the new joint tenants. Your local tax assessor can provide more advice on this issue.

Summary

There are cases in which tenancy arrangements can make sense, from the perspectives of avoiding probate and ensuring that property ownership remains with the targeted person. However, be aware that some of these arrangements can result in the transfer of a partial interest in an asset to the other party during your lifetime, so consult an attorney to evaluate all possible scenarios that might arise.

Chapter 8
The Pay-on-Death Option

Introduction

Besides the asset transfer options noted in the preceding chapters, we present an additional option in this chapter, which is the pay-on-death transfer.

The Pay-on-Death Option

As the name implies, the pay-on-death option allows you to specify which assets someone will receive upon your death. Taking this approach avoids the probate process; instead, the named asset can be transferred at once to the named person. This designation is not stated in your will. Instead, the designation is directly attached to the targeted asset.

The pay-on-death option is most commonly applied to bank accounts, brokerage accounts, stocks, and bonds. In some states, it is also possible to set up a transfer-on-death registration for a vehicle. In fewer states, it is possible to transfer real estate on your death.

The process of setting up the pay-on-death option is usually quite simple. For example, if the assignment relates to a bank account, the bank will provide you with a pay-on-death form to fill out. The bank will retain the form, and will pay the designated beneficiary when it is notified of your death. In the case of a bank account, the beneficiary receives whatever is in the account when you die and that person presents the bank with a death certificate; there is no obligation to set aside a specific sum for the person.

EXAMPLE

Allen Jarvis wants to leave all the cash in his bank account to his daughter, Ashley. To do so, he sets up the account as "Allen Jarvis, depositor, as trustee for Ashley Jarvis, beneficiary". Upon his death, Ashley gives a bank officer a copy of Allen's death certificate and proof of her identity, and then withdraws the entire balance from the account.

You can specify multiple beneficiaries on a pay-on-death account. If so, the bank will pay an equal share of the ending balance to each of the stated beneficiaries. If you specify a minor as the beneficiary, it will be necessary to name a custodian as the payee; this person is then responsible for using the funds in the best interests of the minor.

EXAMPLE

Chris wants to make his grand-daughter Danielle the pay-on-death recipient of his bank account. Danielle is currently eight years old, so Chris names her mother Elinor as the custodian of the account. On the bank-provided form, Chris writes "Elinor Davis, as custodian for Danielle Davis under the Iowa Uniform Transfers to Minors Act."

> **Note:** The beneficiary of any pay-on-death arrangement has no right to the asset for as long as you live. You can spend all the money or sell the asset, if that is what you want.

There are several advantages to pay-on-death bank accounts. First, the beneficiary cannot access the funds in the account while you are still alive (which can be a problem under a joint tenancy arrangement). Also, this arrangement is not considered a gift, so it is not subject to the gift tax.

The main problem with a pay-on-death account is that you cannot specify an alternate beneficiary, in case the primary beneficiary is no longer alive when you die. In this situation, all remaining funds in the account will be transferred to the residuary beneficiary stated in your will. Also, the amount in this account is still considered part of your estate, and so will be included in the determination of any estate tax.

> **Tip:** The most likely type of account to use for a pay-on-death arrangement is a savings account, since that account is most likely to contain a substantial amount of cash.

If you have invested in T-Bills (securities issued by the U.S. Treasury Department), then the pay-on-death option can be applied to them. This involves filling out a form in which you register ownership of the T-Bills in your name, followed by "payable on death to [beneficiary name]". Only one beneficiary can be stated on this form.

The same approach applies to a brokerage account. Your brokerage can supply you with the necessary form, and will deliver the securities in your account to the stated beneficiary upon your death. If your brokerage does not offer this option, then you can always switch to a different brokerage that is willing to provide this service.

It is possible in some states to use the transfer-on-death option for a car registration. If this is available, contact the department of motor vehicles for your state to obtain the applicable form. This option is expanding among the states, but is currently an option in a minority of them.

Finally, it is possible in some states to transfer real estate by a pay-on-death arrangement. If available, you will need to write up a deed and have it notarized and properly filed at the applicable county land records office. The exact requirements vary by state, so if you own property in multiple states, you will need to follow different requirements to complete a pay-on-death deed for each property.

Summary

The transfer-on-death option is a good way to avoid probate, putting property in the hands of your beneficiaries as soon as possible after your death. However, it is not available in all states, so you may need to use other property transfer devices, such as a living trust or joint tenancy.

Chapter 9
Life Insurance Options

Introduction

Life insurance pays out a sum of money following the death of the insured person. It is not always part of a person's estate plan, but can be useful in certain circumstances, as discussed in the following pages.

When to Use Life Insurance

The primary use of life insurance is to pay for the living expenses of a spouse or your children. This is a particular concern when your spouse does not work or earns a significantly lower wage than you, as well as when the children are still many years from becoming adults, when they can support themselves. An additional use of life insurance is that it can provide the cash needed to pay for any debts outstanding at the time of your death, as well as to pay any estate taxes. In these situations, a relatively large-value policy will be needed.

> **Tip:** It is easy to change the beneficiaries on a life insurance policy – just contact your insurance agent and fill out the appropriate form. This is useful when there are changes in your family, such as a divorce or remarriage.

> **Tip:** If you designate a minor as the beneficiary of a life insurance policy, be sure to arrange for a guardian at the same time. Otherwise, the insurer will ask the relevant court to appoint a guardian before it releases the associated funds.

A particularly good use for life insurance is when you have a large estate that will be subject to estate taxes, and which is comprised of mostly non-liquid assets (such as your ownership interest in a business). In these cases, it may be necessary to sell the non-liquid assets quickly, in order to pay the estate taxes. To give your beneficiaries the option to retain control over your assets, it makes sense to obtain sufficient life insurance to pay the expected amount of the estate taxes. Conversely, if the estate already has sufficient cash on hand to pay estate taxes, then there will be no need for life insurance to deal with this issue.

Another possible use for life insurance arises when you own a business, and it depends on you for a large part of its cash flow (perhaps because you are great at sales!). If you want the business to stay in operation after your death, consider how much additional cash it will need to stay in operation until a replacement for you can be found. Or, think about how much cash it will need until a buyer can be found for the business. This should constitute the amount of life insurance you will need.

At a lesser level, life insurance is useful when you are cash poor. In this situation, there might not be enough cash to pay for your funeral or other needs that may arise immediately after your death. In this situation, a relatively small-value policy should be sufficient. However, if most of your property will avoid probate and go directly to your designated heirs, then it may be possible for them to liquidate the assets quickly in order to obtain the necessary cash. Conversely, if your estate will be tied up in probate, then having some extra cash for your beneficiaries presents a reasonable case for acquiring some life insurance.

> **Note:** An advantage of life insurance is that the eventual payout by the insurer does not go through probate, because the policy specifically names a beneficiary.

Conversely, if your situation does not fall into the classifications just stated, then there is no need for life insurance. For example, the typical person whose children have grown up and whose estate falls below the estate tax threshold has no need for life insurance. If there is a limited need for life insurance, then only purchase enough for the indicated need; otherwise, you are wasting money on this insurance.

Varieties of Life Insurance

There are two main types of life insurance. A term policy only provides coverage for a set amount of time, while there are several varieties of permanent insurance that cannot be cancelled by the insurer, unless the associated premiums are not paid on time. It is possible to purchase both term and permanent insurance with a single up-front lump sum payment.

The essential concept behind term life insurance is that it pays out a specific amount of cash if you die during the predefined period when the policy is still in force. It is also the least expensive form of life insurance, since it provides no other benefit. It is relatively inexpensive to obtain if you are young, since the probability of your death is quite low at that time. Consequently, it is an excellent choice when you are young and have young children to protect. As you get older, the price of term insurance increases, since the risk of your death goes up with age. Given the gradual increase in the cost of this insurance, people tend to drop coverage as they age.

EXAMPLE

Wilma purchases a term life insurance policy that will pay out $250,000 if she dies within the next ten years. She dies ten years and one day later, so the policy is no longer in force and the insurer is not obligated to pay out any funds.

A permanent insurance policy automatically rolls forward year after year. The amount you pay for the policy each year is the same. Given that the risk of a payout increases for the insurer each year, you are paying more than would be the case with a term insurance policy during the early years of a permanent policy, and less than would be required for a term insurance policy later in life. The early excess payment is invested by the insurer in order to generate returns that can be used to pay for the eventual payout. Or, if you choose to end the policy, you can obtain this excess amount, which is known as its *cash surrender value*. If the returns on excess policy payments are left with the insurer, then they are not taxable. Conversely, if you choose to cash in the policy, then the cash surrender value is subject to tax.

There are three variations on the permanent insurance concept, which are as follows:

- *Whole life insurance*. This is the most basic type of permanent insurance, providing a fixed amount of uncancellable coverage in exchange for the same payment amount, year after year.
- *Universal life insurance*. This is the same as whole life insurance, but also provides some flexibility in altering the amount of the premiums paid and the death benefit.
- *Variable life insurance*. This has the same benefits as universal life insurance, but also lets you invest in a variety of investment options. The value of your policy may fluctuate as the value of your chosen investments change over time, which means that the associated death benefit could change substantially.

A variation on the life insurance concept is the *first-to-die policy*. Under this arrangement, several people are insured under one policy, with the insurer paying out when the first person dies. This is useful for business partnerships, where the surviving partners need the cash to buy out the beneficiaries' interest in the business. Alternatively, the funds could be used to hire people to replace the owner who has died. It is most common for the business to pay for the related insurance premiums, rather than the insured parties.

EXAMPLE

Able, Bascom and Chanteria start up a new business. Their partnership agreement mandates that, in the event of the death of one of them, the other two partners can buy out the interest of that person. The firm has little excess cash, since it is using all available funds to expand the business. To deal with this situation, the business purchases a first-to-die policy that covers the three of them. The firm acquires sufficient coverage to pay off double the share of one partner, on the assumption that the value of the business will double. Bascom dies five years later, so the insurer pays the business the full amount of the policy. Able and Chanteria use the money to buy out Bascom's interest in the firm, paying his beneficiaries. There is some residual cash from the policy, which is retained as working capital. Able and Chanteria are now 50-50 owners of the business.

Tip: Do not select an insurance policy on your own. Find a trustworthy insurance agent who can walk you through the massive array of options to find one that matches your exact estate planning needs.

Another variation on the life insurance concept is an annuity. Under this arrangement, the insurer pays the beneficiary a fixed amount at regular intervals, such as once a month. This concept is most useful when the beneficiary is more likely to spend funds excessively. Spreading out payments to this person makes it less likely that he or she will waste the funds.

Transferring Policy Ownership

In those rare cases in which your estate is large enough to be subject to the federal estate tax, it can make sense to transfer the ownership of your life insurance policies to another party. If you own or have any control[4] over the policy at the time of your death, then the proceeds from the insurance are included in the calculation of your estate. Conversely, if policy ownership can be shifted elsewhere, then the proceeds are not included in your estate.

Note: If the policy proceeds are payable to your spouse, then they are not subject to the federal estate tax.

Transferring policy ownership is allowable, as long as the insurer has a record of the transfer (usually on one of its own transfer forms, specifying that the insured party is no longer the owner). You can assign ownership to any adult, which may include the beneficiary of the policy. However, you will lose all control over the policy once it has been transferred, so you will no longer be able to cancel the policy or alter the beneficiary. Consequently, it makes the most sense to only transfer the ownership of a life insurance policy to someone you trust implicitly.

Tip: If you are going to transfer ownership of a life insurance policy, do it while you are still healthy, since the IRS will disallow the transfer if it occurs within three years of your death.

The act of transferring a life insurance policy to someone else creates a taxable gift. This means that a gift tax will be assessed on the present value of the policy, subject to the gift tax rules stated in a later chapter. This is still likely to be a good deal, since the proceeds to be gained from the policy are usually far less when you are alive than the much larger payout after you have died.

---

[4] You are considered to still have control over a life insurance policy if you can cancel it, change the beneficiary, borrow against it, or change the manner in which policy payments are made.

EXAMPLE

Andrea transfers the ownership of her life insurance policy to her daughter Willie. On the day she authorizes the transfer, the cash surrender value of the policy is $35,000. Andrea dies five years later, at which point the insurer pays Willie $500,000, which is the policy payout. Neither amount is included in Andrea's estate, and Willie pays taxes on the cash surrender value of the policy.

The downside for the person receiving the gift of an insurance policy is that this person should now make all scheduled premium payments. Otherwise, if you were to keep making payments, then the IRS could make a strong case that you still control the policy, so the policy payout should be included in your estate.

Another way to transfer policy ownership is to park it in an irrevocable life insurance trust. This involves creating the trust and then transferring the policy into this entity. Since the trust now owns the policy, it is no longer part of your estate, and so is not subject to the estate tax. This approach has the advantage of giving you better control over the policy, thereby avoiding the risk of having someone else gain control and alter the terms of the policy – as might occur if you were to gift it to someone.

EXAMPLE

George is the widowed father of two daughters, neither of whom has any sense with money. He has a whole life insurance policy that will pay out $3 million when he dies, as well as millions in other assets. He wants to minimize his estate taxes while also ensuring that the daughters do not spend the money coming from the insurance policy in a profligate manner. George asks a trusted friend to be the trustee of a life insurance trust, to which he transfers the policy. Following George's death, the friend will administer the money for his daughters in accordance with George's wishes, as stated in the trust documentation.

A life insurance trust is only considered valid by the IRS if you are not the trustee, it is irrevocable (you can't revoke it), and it was established at least three years prior to your death. Otherwise, the IRS will disregard the existence of the trust and assume that the life insurance proceeds are part of your estate.

Summary

Life insurance tends to be more necessary earlier in your life, when your children are still minors. Once they become adults and can earn a living themselves, there is less need for life insurance. It is also less of a concern once you have retired, and presumably have built up a fairly large cash reserve. Consequently, it makes sense to periodically review your life insurance situation and adjust the amount of your life insurance policies.

Chapter 10
Retirement Plans

Introduction

Upon your retirement, you might qualify for payments from one or more retirement plans. The most likely is social security, while you may also receive payments from a company pension plan, an individual retirement account, a 401(k) account, and so forth. Part of estate planning addresses the amount and timing of these payments. For example, if you and your spouse will both be the recipients of generous retirement plan payments, this gives you more room to transfer substantial gifts to family members or charities prior to your death. As another example, the absence of a significant pension might improve the desirability of taking out a life insurance policy on one spouse, so that the other spouse will have sufficient cash to live on if the first spouse dies first.

Social Security Benefits

Workers who have paid into the federal government's social security system for at least 10 years become eligible for early retirement benefits at age 62. If you wait until your full retirement age (between 66 and 67, depending on when you were born), this results in greater monthly benefits. Delaying the collection of retirement benefits to age 70 results in even larger payments.

Spouses can also claim benefits, based on either their own earnings or their spouse's. A divorced spouse who is not still married can receive benefits based on a prior spouse's earnings if the marriage lasted for at least ten years.

The amount you receive as a social security retirement benefit depends on your average indexed monthly earnings during your 35 highest-earning years. Because of this basis of calculation, the amounts paid will differ by retiree. The annual amount paid to you increases by 8% for each year in which you delay collecting benefits, starting at age 62 and stopping at age 70. This means that the benefit varies, depending on when you start taking it. In addition, there is an annual cost-of-living adjustment to social security benefits. In 2023, the maximum monthly benefit for those aged 62 was $2,572 (which is $30,864 on an annual basis), while for those aged 70 it was $4,555 (which is $54,660 on an annual basis).

The spouse and children of a deceased person may be eligible for survivor benefits, based on the person's earnings record. The surviving spouse is eligible if he or she is 60 or older, or 50 or older and disabled, provided that there has been no remarriage. In addition, a surviving spouse who is caring for a minor that is younger than 16 or disabled may also qualify for survivor benefits.

Individual Retirement Accounts

An individual retirement account is also referred to as a traditional IRA. This is an account that a person creates, and into which he or she can contribute the lower of total annual compensation or (as of 2024) $7,000 per year, or $8,000 for those at least 50 years old. Depending upon the circumstances, these contributions may be tax deductible for those employees with lower compensation levels. In addition, any income earned on the funds invested in it is shielded from taxation until withdrawn. A person can begin withdrawing funds from the account as of age 59½, and is required to begin doing so as of age 73. If a person does not withdraw the minimum required amount as of age 73, the penalty for not doing so is 50% of the amount that should have been withdrawn.

Roth IRA

A Roth IRA is similar to a traditional IRA account, except that the participant pays taxes on funds when they are contributed to the account, rather than when the funds are later withdrawn. By doing so, all interest earned subsequent to placing funds in the account is tax-free. A participant can withdraw funds from the account as of age 59½. Since there is no subsequent taxation of the earnings in a Roth IRA, there is no reason for the government to require participants to draw down these funds, so there is no minimum draw down, as was the case for a traditional IRA. Instead, no withdrawal is required from this account until the death of the owner. Once the account owner dies, the same minimum distribution rules that apply to traditional IRAs also apply to Roth IRAs.

IRA and Roth IRA Comparison

Some of the differences and similarities between traditional and Roth IRAs are noted in the following exhibit.

Comparison of Traditional and Roth IRAs

Features	Traditional IRA	Roth IRA
Who is allowed to contribute?	Anyone with taxable compensation	Anyone with taxable compensation and a modified adjusted gross income below a predetermined cap
Can contributions be deducted?	Qualifying contributions are deductible	Contributions are not deductible
How much can be contributed?	The combined amount for both IRAs is the smaller of $6,500 (or $7,500 for someone age 50 or older), or one's taxable compensation for the year.	
What is the contribution deadline?	The tax return filing deadline, not including any extensions.	
When can money be withdrawn?	Money can be withdrawn at any time.	

Features	Traditional IRA	Roth IRA
Is a minimum distribution required?	The account owner must begin taking distributions by April 1 following the year in which he or she turned age 73, and by December 31 of subsequent years.	Not required for the original owner of the account.
Are withdrawals taxable?	All deductible contributions and earnings that are withdrawn are taxable. If a withdrawal is made prior to age 59½, a 10% tax may be imposed.	A qualified distribution is not taxable. A distribution is qualified when it is made after the five-year period beginning with the first tax year for which a contribution was made to the account, *and* the distribution was made after reaching age 59½, or was made due to being disabled, or for a first-time home purchase, or was made to a beneficiary or estate due to the account owner's death. Otherwise, a 10% tax may be imposed.

Rollover IRA

When an employee leaves a business where he or she has funds in a qualified pension plan, the best options are to either leave the funds in the plan, roll them into the qualified plan of the new employer, or roll them into a rollover IRA. This last option is an IRA account that is specifically designed to accept funds from qualified pension plans. Since many people have multiple employers during their careers, many with qualified pension plans, it makes sense to consolidate the funds in these accounts into a rollover IRA.

Savings Incentive Match Plan for Employees (SIMPLE)

As the acronym implies, this is a simplified retirement plan under which both the employer and employee can make contributions to an IRA account. It is funded through a pre-tax reduction of employee gross pay. The maximum annual contribution to a SIMPLE account (as of 2024) was $16,500 and $20,000 for those at least 50 years old. A SIMPLE plan can only be created by an employer having fewer than 100 employees, or which has employed an average of 100 or fewer employees in either of the two preceding years. If a business subsequently increases its employment, it can still operate a SIMPLE plan as long as it does not employ an average of 100 or more people in a subsequent year. This plan requires the employer to match each employee's salary reduction contribution on a dollar-for-dollar basis up to 3% of the employee's compensation. A variation is the nonelective contribution, where the employer can choose to make a 2%-of-compensation contribution on behalf of each eligible employee, even if the employees do not elect to make a salary deduction into their IRA accounts.

Simplified Employee Pension (SEP) IRA

A SEP IRA is designed for the self-employed person, but can be extended to all types of business entities. A SEP IRA can only be created if there is no qualified retirement plan already in place. Contributions to a SEP IRA are protected from income taxes until such time as they are withdrawn from the account. Participants may begin withdrawing funds from the account as of age 59½, and must make required minimum distributions once they reach age 72. The total contribution to a SEP IRA cannot exceed the lesser of 25% of a participant's annual compensation or $69,000 (as of 2024). These contribution levels make the SEP IRA one of the best ways to protect a substantial amount of funds from taxation.

EXAMPLE

Martha earned $48,000 in 2024. The maximum contribution she can make to her SEP IRA is $12,000 (calculated as 25% × $48,000).

EXAMPLE

Mary earned $300,000 in 2024. The maximum contribution she can make to her SEP IRA is $69,000, since that is the maximum allowable contribution for 2024.

Rollover Options

It might be useful to shift the balance in another investment vehicle into an IRA, or to shift funds out of an IRA and into a different investment vehicle. We discuss these concepts in the following paragraphs.

It is usually possible to roll over the balance in a workplace retirement account to an IRA. The only situations in which this is not allowed are as follows:

- A distribution that is one of a series of substantially equal payments
- Distributions of excess contributions and related earnings
- Distributions paid for accident, health or life insurance
- Dividends on employer securities
- Hardship distributions
- Loans classified as deemed distributions
- Required minimum distributions
- S corporation allocations treated as deemed distributions
- Withdrawals electing out of automatic contribution arrangements

Conversely, it is possible to roll over the balance in an IRA to a qualified retirement plan (such as a 401(k) plan) if the receiving plan allows it to accept such a rollover.

A traditional IRA can be converted to a Roth IRA by receiving a distribution from the IRA and contributing it to a Roth IRA within 60 days. Alternatively, the trustee holding the IRA can be instructed to transfer the funds directly to the trustee of the

Roth IRA account. This conversion results in taxation of any untaxed amounts in the traditional IRA.

It is also possible to roll over the balance from one traditional IRA into another traditional IRA, as long as the funds are reinvested in the receiving IRA within 60 days. The rollover is only tax-free if the property being contributed to the receiving IRA is the same property received from the distributing IRA. A further rule is that a person can only make one rollover from an IRA to another IRA in any one-year period. However, there is no such limitation on trustee-to-trustee transfers. Also, there is no limitation on rollovers from traditional IRAs to Roth IRAs.

Tip: If an eligible rollover distribution is paid directly to you, the payer must withhold 20% of it, even if you plan to roll it over into a traditional IRA. This can be avoided by taking the direct rollover option, where the funds are sent directly to a traditional IRA.

Required Minimum Distributions

A minimum withdrawal is required for a traditional IRA, SIMPLE IRA and SEP IRA by April 1 of the year following the calendar year in which the account owner reaches age 73. This age is reduced to 70½ years for those born before July 1, 1949. The basic rules associated with these withdrawals are as follows:

- It is allowable to withdraw more than the minimum required amount.
- There is no exception from the required minimum withdrawals for those who are still working.
- Withdrawals must be included in taxable income except for any funds that had already been taxed, or which can be received tax-free. No withdrawal is required from a Roth IRA account until the death of the owner, since the funds placed in the account were already taxed.
- Subsequent withdrawals must be made by December 31 of each year. For the first year following the year when an account owner reaches the triggering age a distribution is required by April 1, followed by another withdrawal by December 31.

EXAMPLE

Emily reaches age 73 on September 15, 2023. She must receive her 2023 required minimum distribution by April 1, 2024, based on her 2023 year-end balance. Emily must receive her 2024 required minimum distribution by December 31, 2024, based on her 2024 year-end balance.

The required minimum distribution in each year is the account balance at the end of the immediately preceding calendar year, divided by the distribution period stated on the IRS's Uniform Lifetime Table for the account owner's age. This table is used for unmarried account owners, married owners whose spouses are not more than 10 years younger, and married owners whose spouses are not the sole beneficiaries of their IRAs. Distributions reduce the account balance in the year they are made. Thus, a distribution for 2023 made after December 31 of 2024 reduces the account balance for 2024, not 2023. The Uniform Lifetime Table appears in the following exhibit. In deciding whether to use the table, marital status is determined as of January 1 of each year; any divorce or death is disregarded until the following year.

Uniform Lifetime Table

Age	Distribution Period	Age	Distribution Period
72	27.4	95	8.9
73	26.5	96	8.4
74	25.5	97	7.8
75	24.6	98	7.3
76	23.7	99	6.8
77	22.9	100	6.4
78	22.0	101	6.0
79	21.1	102	5.6
80	20.2	103	5.2
81	19.4	104	4.9
82	18.5	105	4.6
83	17.7	106	4.3
84	16.8	107	4.1
85	16.0	108	3.9
86	15.2	109	3.7
87	14.4	110	3.5
88	13.7	111	3.4
89	12.9	112	3.3
90	12.2	113	3.1
91	11.5	114	3.0
92	10.8	115	2.9
93	10.1	116	2.8
94	9.5	117+	2.7

EXAMPLE

Francis owns a traditional IRA. His account balance at the end of 2024 was $200,000. His sole beneficiary is his spouse, who is two years younger. Francis will be 80 years old in 2024. According to the Uniform Lifetime Table, his distribution period is 20.2. Therefore, his required distribution amount is $9,901 (calculated as $200,000 ÷ 20.2).

If a beneficiary is the account owner's surviving spouse and sole designated beneficiary, then this person will also use the Uniform Lifetime Table to calculate required minimum distributions. However, if the account owner had not yet reached age 73 when he or she died, and the beneficiary elected not to be treated as the owner of the IRA, then the beneficiary does not have to take any distributions until the year in which the account owner would have reached age 73.

Table I (Single Life Expectancy) is used by beneficiaries who are not the spouse of the account owner, while Table II (Joint Life and Last Survivor Expectancy) is intended for owners whose spouses are more than 10 years younger, and are the account owner's sole beneficiaries. Table I appears in the following exhibit.

Table I, Single Life Expectancy (for use by beneficiaries)

Age	Life Expectancy	Age	Life Expectancy	Age	Life Expectancy	Age	Life Expectancy
0	84.6	28	57.3	56	30.6	84	8.7
1	83.7	29	56.3	57	29.8	85	8.1
2	82.8	30	55.3	58	28.9	86	7.6
3	81.8	31	54.4	59	28.0	87	7.1
4	80.8	32	53.4	60	27.1	88	6.6
5	79.8	33	52.5	61	26.2	89	6.1
6	78.8	34	51.5	62	25.4	90	5.7
7	77.9	35	50.5	63	24.5	91	5.3
8	76.9	36	49.6	64	23.7	92	4.9
9	75.9	37	48.6	65	22.9	93	4.6
10	74.9	38	47.7	66	22.0	94	4.3
11	73.9	39	46.7	67	21.2	95	4.0
12	72.9	40	45.7	68	20.4	96	3.7
13	71.9	41	44.8	69	19.6	97	3.4
14	70.9	42	43.8	70	18.8	98	3.2
15	69.9	43	42.9	71	18.0	99	3.0
16	69.0	44	41.9	72	17.2	100	2.8
17	68.0	45	41.0	73	16.4	101	2.6
18	67.0	46	40.0	74	15.6	102	2.5
19	66.0	47	39.0	75	14.8	103	2.3
20	65.0	48	38.1	76	14.1	104	2.2
21	64.1	49	37.1	77	13.3	105	2.1
22	63.1	50	36.2	78	12.6	106	2.1
23	62.1	51	35.3	79	11.9	107	2.1
24	61.1	52	34.3	80	11.2	108	2.0
25	60.2	53	33.4	81	10.5	109	2.0
26	59.2	54	32.5	82	9.9	110	2.0
27	58.2	55	31.6	83	9.3	111+	2.0

EXAMPLE

Mary is the surviving spouse and the sole designated beneficiary. Her husband, Jonathan, would have been 73 years old in 2024, so distributions will begin in 2024. Mary becomes 67 years old in 2023. She uses Table I, Single Life Expectancy, to determine her distribution period, which is 21.2.

Qualified Charitable Distributions

A qualified charitable distribution is a distribution from an IRA that would otherwise have been taxable, which is paid directly to a qualified charity. A further requirement is that the qualified charity must issue an acknowledgement of the contribution that would normally be issued for a donor to claim a deduction for a charitable donation. These distributions can be used to satisfy the required minimum distribution from an IRA. A qualified charity is one that is eligible to receive tax-free donations.

EXAMPLE

Charity Do-Right (sister of Dudley) is required to make a $7,000 required minimum distribution from her IRA in the current year. She distributes $6,000 from the IRA directly to a qualified charity, and then has to withdraw another $1,000 to satisfy the minimum distribution requirement.

Defined Contribution Plans

A defined contribution plan is a retirement plan where the employer is responsible for contributing a specific amount into the plan, and is not responsible for the amount of any benefits eventually paid from the plan to participants. This means that the risk associated with subsequent performance of the fund is borne by participants, not the employer. Participants in a defined contribution plan may have a number of different investment options, which have varying risk profiles and possible returns on investment. The more common defined contribution plans are as follows:

- *401(k) plan.* This is an investment account into which employees contribute funds, sometimes with additional matching funds contributed by the employer. The funds contributed by the employer are usually under a vesting arrangement, where the participants earn the funds by staying employed with the company for a certain period of time. Participants pay income taxes on the funds in a 401(k) account when they withdraw funds from the account. The net effect of a 401(k) is to defer the recognition of taxable income until retirement, when participants will presumably also be in a lower tax bracket, and so will pay fewer income taxes. With some hardship-based exceptions, a participant cannot withdraw funds from a 401(k) account until at least age 59½ without facing large penalties. To mitigate this problem for cash-strapped participants, a 401(k) account may provide for loans to participants up to the amount of their contributed funds, and on which they must pay interest.
- *403(b) plan.* This is a plan similar in concept and tax treatment to the 401(k) plan, but designed for public education and non-profit entities.
- *Money purchase plan.* This plan requires the employer to pay into each employee's plan account a percentage of his or her compensation for that year. The payments can be quite substantial, since the contribution cap per year is the lesser of 25% of employee compensation or $69,000 (in 2024). These

payments are treated as deferred income for participants until they withdraw the funds.

- *Profit sharing plan.* This plan is essentially the same as a money purchase plan, except that the employer funds any contributions with a portion of its profits. The amount of payments made is discretionary, and the employer can even choose to make contributions to the plan in the absence of company profits. Contributions are typically made to each participant's account based on his or her annual compensation as a percentage of all compensation among plan participants. The contribution per year per participant is the lesser of 25% of employee compensation or $69,000 (in 2024).

Upon the death of an account holder, the named beneficiary receives the cash left in the account. If the account holder is married, then the person's spouse is the beneficiary – though this person can give up the right to be the beneficiary. Naming your spouse as the beneficiary is a good way to defer estate taxes until the spouse dies.

Summary

The key estate tax issue relating to retirement plans is that any cash left in a retirement account is included in your assets for the purpose of determining any estate tax, no matter how you have arranged to have these funds paid out to a beneficiary. If your spouse inherits the funds in your retirement account, then this money cannot be taxed, because of the unlimited marital deduction. This deduction allows you to transfer an unrestricted amount of assets to your spouse at any time (including at your death), free of tax.

Funds parked in an individual retirement plan were placed there on a tax-deferred basis, so a beneficiary inheriting these funds must pay income tax on them. However, funds parked in a Roth IRA are not taxed when the beneficiary receives the cash, because contributions to this type of plan are not tax deferred; instead, you already paid tax on these funds before placing them in the account.

Chapter 11
Estate Taxes

Introduction

The *estate tax* is levied on the net value of the estate of a deceased person before distribution to the heirs. This is not a concern for the vast majority of taxpayers, because of a very large federal exemption on this tax. The result is that only those with large estates will ever have to worry about paying it. For those in this fortunate situation, we provide estate tax details in the following pages.

Estate Tax Exemptions

When it comes to the estate tax, the key number to be aware of is the federal-level exemption from the tax, which is $13,610,000 in 2024 – per person. Thus, if your estate has a total value of $10 million, then the estate tax does not apply. If your estate has a value of $20 million, then the amount subject to the tax in 2024 is $6,390,000. This exemption is an important consideration, because the federal estate tax can be as high as 40%.

An additional feature of the exemption is that it is applied separately to each person in a married couple, so that the total exemption for a couple is essentially $27,220,000 in 2024. In addition, if there is any unused exemption for one spouse, this amount can be shifted over to the surviving spouse, which increases the survivor's exemption. Also, all property left to the surviving spouse is exempt from estate tax, though it does not apply to spouses who are not citizens of the United States. If a non-citizen spouse becomes a citizen by the time the estate tax must be filed, then the spouse will be entitled to the marriage deduction.

> **Note:** As the name implies, the marital deduction does not apply to unmarried couples. According to estate tax law, it pays to be married.

EXAMPLE

Tommy's estate is valued at $25 million. He leaves $3 million to his children, with the remaining $22 million going to his wife. Because the transfer to his wife is exempt from the federal estate tax, the total value of his estate drops to the $3 million gift to his children, which is well below the federal estate tax threshold. As a result, the estate tax does not apply to his estate at all.

Another exemption worth considering relates to charities. If you leave assets to a tax-exempt charity (one with the 501(c)(3) designation), then these assets are exempt from the estate tax. This exemption can be a considerable inducement to leave a large part of your estate to a favorite charity. Larger charities likely have formal programs to assist you in giving them large payouts from your estate.

There are also a few minor exemptions that can be taken to reduce the value of your estate, such as probate fees, claims against the estate by third parties, and funeral expenses. These exemptions tend not to have much of an impact from the perspective of your planning to minimize estate taxes.

These exemptions make it extremely unlikely that the average taxpayer will ever be in a position to pay the federal estate tax.

Estate Valuation

The net value of an estate (assets minus liabilities) is not something that can be determined with any degree of precision. Instead, you will need to make a rough guess at this value for estate planning purposes. If your estimate is well below the estate tax exemption, then don't worry about the estate valuation any further, because there will be no tax.

An estate's valuation is not based on its book value, but rather its market value on the day of your death, minus any outstanding debts on that date. The person responsible for deriving this valuation is the person in charge of your estate, which may be the trustee of your living trust, the executor of your will, or your surviving spouse – it all depends on the circumstances. If the estate is a large one, it may be necessary for this person to hire a professional appraiser to develop a valuation. An appraiser is especially useful when there are substantial assets that are difficult to value, such as shares in a closely-held business, or works of art. While there is a tax incentive to minimize the value of an estate, be aware that the IRS can challenge this valuation.

Paying the Estate Tax

An estate tax form must be completed and submitted to the IRS when the gross value of your estate exceeds the amount of the personal exemption in the year of your death. Since filing is based on the gross value of your estate (prior to the settlement of any offsetting liabilities), it is quite possible that the form must be filed even though your estate owes no estate tax. The executor is responsible for filing this return, but given the difficulty of the return, it should always be handed off to a tax expert to prepare.

If you suspect that some amount of estate tax will be owed, you might consider specifying in your will (or living trust) which assets are to be liquidated in order to pay the tax. If these assets turn out not to be sufficient to pay the taxes, then you can leave it up to the executor or trustee to sell off additional assets to pay the residual tax. It can be useful to make this specification to keep anyone from conducting a general estate liquidation in order to pay taxes.

If you do not want to pay the federal estate tax, then consider giving away a portion of your estate each year (while still living). There is a cap on how much of these gifts can be made each year, as discussed in the following chapter. Nonetheless, if you have many worthy candidates for gifts, then this is an excellent way to reduce the size of your estate.

> **Tip:** Give away assets during your life that have not appreciated much in value. Retain in your estate any assets that have appreciated substantially, since your beneficiaries will then inherit the market value of these assets at your death, giving them a much higher tax basis in these assets than would otherwise be the case.

Related State Taxes

In addition to the federal government, some states impose inheritance or estate taxes. An inheritance tax is based on the value of a deceased person's property within the state, and is imposed on the beneficiaries, rather than the estate. Tax rates vary widely on inheritance taxes, but tend to be lowest on spouses. A nonrelative receiving property from an estate can expect to pay the highest inheritance tax rate.

Alternatively, a state might impose an inheritance tax, which might be payable even if the estate owes no tax to the federal government. This is because the exemption levels tend to be much lower at the state level – sometimes as low as $1 million. Consequently, there is a good chance that a person with a moderate-sized estate will be subject to the estate tax in the state in which he or she resides. If you feel that this tax will be onerous, a possible option is to move out of the state and into one that does not impose a large estate tax.

> **Tip:** If you elect to move to a different state, be sure to make it quite clear that you have in fact moved. This means voting in the state to which you move, shifting your bank and brokerage accounts to that state, and residing there the majority of the time. Otherwise, your old state might claim that you were domiciled there when you died, and attempt to impose inheritance or estate taxes.

Summary

The central issue with estate taxes is whether your estate is below the threshold estate tax exemption level. If so, and especially if there is no indication that you are likely to exceed it in the future, then any planning to avoid paying the tax is a waste of time.

Chapter 12
Gift Taxes

Introduction

Gifting assets to other parties is an excellent way to reduce the amount of estate taxes owed. As long as the amounts paid out are relatively small, there is no tax, nor any reporting requirement. However, when an individual pays out larger amounts, it will be necessary to complete IRS Form 709, *United States Gift Tax Return*, and it may be necessary to pay a gift tax. In this chapter, we discuss the nature of the gift tax, when gifts must be reported, and how to avoid the tax.

The Gift Tax

The *gift tax* is a federal tax that is imposed on a donor who gives something of value to another person while the donor is still living, where the donor gives up all control over the transferred asset. For something to be considered a gift, the receiving party cannot pay full value for the gift, though some lesser amount may be paid. If a lesser amount is paid, the difference between the value of the gift and the value of the consideration provided is the amount of the gift.

The gift tax may also apply to forgiving a debt, to making an interest-free or below-market interest rate loan, and to transferring the benefits of an insurance policy. Further, the tax applies to any digital asset, such as an electronic record, data stored in a binary format, virtual currency, digital images, and domain names.

The effective date of a gift is when the donor no longer has control over the asset in question. This is the point at which the donor can no longer revoke the gift.

EXAMPLE

Mrs. Fields delivers a stock certificate for 1,000 shares of International Cookie Company, properly endorsed, to her grandson Chip. This gift is complete as soon as it is delivered.

EXAMPLE

Mr. Jones, the donor, signs a check for $8,000 made out to his daughter Emily, which constitutes a promise to pay. This gift is not complete until the check has been cashed by Emily.

The tax was created to deter taxpayers from giving assets to other parties in order to avoid paying estate taxes. Otherwise, a person possessing substantial wealth could simply transfer large amounts of it to children and grandchildren prior to his or her death.

The gift tax can be substantial, depending on the amount of the gift. A small gift may have a modest 18% tax assigned to it, while a large one could be assigned a 40%

tax. This tax is paid on that portion of an estate that exceeds the lifetime exclusion amount (as explained shortly).

Who Pays Gift Tax

In those cases in which a gift tax is owed, it is paid by the party *giving* the gift, not the recipient. This is done in order to avoid undue hardship on the recipient, who may not have received liquid assets as part of a gift, and so might have a difficult time coming up with the cash to pay the tax.

The Gift Tax Exclusion

There are a number of exceptions to which the gift tax does not apply. The following are all exceptions:

- *Gifts to the donor's spouse.* If the spouse is a United States citizen, the amount that can be gifted tax-free is unlimited. If the spouse is not a citizen, then there is an annual cap of $175,000 on tax-free gifts.
- *Gifts to a political organization.* Gifts made to organizations classified by the IRS as political organizations are not subject to gift tax.
- *Tuition expenditures.* Payments made to a *qualifying educational institution*[5] on behalf of another party for tuition are not subject to gift tax. These payments must be made straight to the educational institution, not the donee. Also, any expenditures made for room and board or books are not eligible for this exclusion. Any non-tuition payments made to an educational institution are considered a gift to the person for whose benefit it was made.
- *Medical expenditures.* Payments made to a health care provider on behalf of another party for medical care are not subject to gift tax. Medical care includes expenses incurred for the diagnosis, cure, mitigation, treatment, or prevention of disease, or for transportation for medical care. It also includes amounts paid for medical insurance on behalf of someone else.
- *Gifts to charitable organizations.* Gifts made to organizations classified by the IRS as charitable organizations are not subject to gift tax. Examples of such entities are educational and religious institutions.
- *Gifts under the exclusion rate.* Gifts under the annual gift-tax exclusion rate are tax-free. When a gift exceeds $17,000, the first $17,000 is not included in the aggregate amount of the donor's taxable gifts within that year.

The last of these bullet points is the most commonly used exclusion. When a gift is for an amount lower than the annual gift tax exclusion rate, then there is no tax; such gifts are said to be excluded from the gift tax. There are two types of exclusions, which are annual and lifetime.

---

[5] A qualifying educational institution is one that normally maintains a regular faculty and curriculum and normally has a regularly enrolled body of students in attendance at the place where its educational activities are carried on.

EXAMPLE

Gregory is highly supportive of his son's decision to go to flight school, so that he can receive training for a commercial pilot's license. To show his support, Gregory pays the flight school $30,000 for the first year's tuition. In addition, and in the same year, Gregory gives his son $12,000 to cover textbooks and housing costs. Neither one of these payments is subject to gift tax, because the tuition is an excluded item and the $12,000 payment falls within the annual exclusion limit.

If Gregory had instead sent his son the entire $42,000, allowing him to use $30,000 of the amount to pay tuition, then Gregory would have had to report $25,000 of gift payments (with the remaining $17,000 falling under the annual exclusion). This would have reduced his lifetime exclusion (as explained in a following section) from $12.92 million to $12.895 million.

The Annual Exclusion

The annual exclusion is currently set at $17,000. This means that a donor can give another person up to $17,000 per year without having to pay any gift tax. This exclusion is per recipient, not per donor, which means that a donor could gift up to $17,000 to a number of different recipients without triggering any gift tax liability.

> **Note:** There is no limit on the number of donees to which a donor can issue gifts. Thus, the $17,000 exclusion can be multiplied by any number of recipients, without limit.

EXAMPLE

A multi-millionaire gives the commencement address at a very small local college. During his address, he announces that he will pay every graduating person $10,000. Since there are 300 graduates, he has just promised to pay $3,000,000 – all of which is excluded from the gift tax.

The Lifetime Exclusion

The lifetime exclusion is the grand total that a donor can give over his or her life without paying any gift tax. This amount is adjusted for inflation each year, and currently stands at $12,920,000. Thus, a donor could gift $12,920,000 over the course of his or her life before having to pay any gift tax. The annual exclusion still applies each year; the lifetime exclusion represents a second cap, which applies to amounts exceeding the annual exclusion.

If a donor gifts more than the annual maximum (currently $17,000) to a single recipient, the donor will not necessarily owe any gift tax, since the excess may still be less than the lifetime gift tax exclusion amount. However, even if this is the case, the donor will need to report the gift on IRS Form 709 (as discussed later in this chapter).

EXAMPLE

Mary Dunton gives $18,000 each to six relatives, for a total of $108,000. Because the annual exclusion is currently set at $17,000 per person, $102,000 of this amount is not subject to gift tax (though the remaining $6,000 is subject to the tax). The non-excluded $6,000 reduces her lifetime exclusion from $12.92 million to $12.914 million.

The Value of a Gift

When property is given as a gift, its value is the fair market value of the property on the transfer date. In this context, fair market value is the price that a buyer is willing to pay and at which a seller is willing to sell, where there is no compulsion to buy or sell and both parties have a reasonable knowledge of the facts. Fair market value should not be derived from a forced sale (such as a bankruptcy sale), since the price tends to be quite low in a forced sale. A few additional points in regard to determining fair market value are as follows:

- *Real estate.* Use the sale prices of properties that share as many characteristics of the real estate being gifted as possible on the date of the transfer.
- *Securities.* Use the average between the highest and lowest quoted selling prices of the securities being gifted on the date of the transfer.
- *Tangible assets.* Use the sale prices of tangible assets that share as many characteristics of the asset being gifted as possible on the date of transfer.

EXAMPLE

Erica buys a new dining room set and gives her old furniture to her son, Doug. The old furniture turns out to be antique, and so has quite a reasonable market value of $29,000. Erica should report the $29,000 value on Form 709.

The proper valuation of a gift is important, because the IRS can impose an under-assessment penalty when a gift tax is underpaid due to a substantial under-assessment. The IRS considers a substantial valuation understatement to have occurred when the value claimed for an asset turns out to be 65% or less than its correct valuation. A gross valuation understatement occurs when the reported value of a gifted asset is 40% or less of its actual value. However, if a gift tax underpayment is in an amount less than $1,000, no penalty will be assessed. Further, the IRS may not assess the penalty in cases where the donor can show that the valuation used was made in good faith, and that he or she had a reasonable basis for the valuation.

The Present Interest Concept

We will make note of the present interest concept in a later section on gift tax minimization strategies. The beneficiary of an asset donation will receive either a present interest or future interest in the asset. A *present interest* is present when the beneficiary obtains an unrestricted right to the immediate use or enjoyment of the asset or the income derived from it. Someone with a present interest in an asset can keep other parties from using it.

Conversely, a *future interest* is present when the beneficiary obtains a similar right, but which will be triggered at a future date. A future interest is most common in a trust arrangement where the beneficiary may not obtain access to or ownership of an asset for an extended period of time.

The distinction between present and future interests is essential, because a beneficiary must have a present interest in a gifted asset before the gift can qualify for the annual gift tax exclusion.

EXAMPLE

Wayne makes an outright gift of a used backhoe to his friend Alfred. The backhoe has a fair market value of $12,000 on the date of transfer. Alfred can use the backhoe or sell it immediately, which indicates that he has a present interest in the gift.

EXAMPLE

Alice transfers assets in a trust with a life estate to Jeremy, with income from the trust to be paid to Jeremy once a year. The trust is structured so that the remainder interest transfers to Harold, Jeremy's son, when Jeremy dies. In this case, the gift made by Alice to Jeremy has a present interest, while the gift made to Harold has a future interest.

The gift of a future interest in an asset cannot be excluded under the annual exclusion.

Note: The gift of a bond or similar instrument that does not pay any interest until maturity is still considered a gift of a present interest. Also, bonds that are exempt from federal income taxes are not exempt from federal gift taxes.

A gift to a minor is considered a present interest only if all of the following conditions are present:

- Both the property and its income may be expended by, or for the benefit of, the minor before the person reaches age 21;
- All remaining property and its income must pass to the minor on the minor's 21st birthday; and
- If the minor dies before the age of 21, the property and its income will be payable either to the minor's estate or to whomever the minor may appoint under a general power of appointment.

Gift Tax Minimization Strategies

There are several techniques available for minimizing the gift tax, and perhaps to avoid it entirely. These alternatives are noted in the following sub-sections.

Gift Splitting

The annual exclusion applies to the amount that one person gifts to another party. This means that spouses can each give $17,000 to the same recipient, for a total of $34,000 per year, as long as both spouses consent to the arrangement. This means that a married couple can effectively double the gift sent to the same person each year – without triggering the gift tax. However, this gift splitting concept only applies if each spouse is a citizen or resident of the United States (thus, gift splitting does not apply when one spouse is a nonresident alien). Also, a person is only considered a spouse if he or she is married to the other donor at the time of the gift and does not remarry during the remainder of the calendar year.

When a couple lives in a community property state, it is unnecessary to formally split a gift. This is because each spouse owns a one-half interest in the property. Therefore, a couple that gifts community property does not need to file a gift tax return on a $34,000 gift to a donee.

EXAMPLE

Mr. and Mrs. Dingle make a gift of $100,000 of community property. This is considered a gift of $50,000 made by each spouse. Therefore, each spouse must file a gift tax return.

This gift splitting strategy is commonly used by wealthier couples to transfer significant amounts of wealth to their children and other relatives through a multi-year program of gift giving. This strategy works especially well when the donors also pay tuition directly to the school or college to which a grandchild is sent, since these payments are exempted from the gift tax.

Gift in Trust – General

There is no gift tax impact when a grantor moves assets into a revocable trust, because the transfer is incomplete. In this situation, the grantor can revoke the trust at will, so the assets cannot yet be considered a gift. Only when assets are distributed from a revocable trust does the IRS consider a gift to have been made.

When a grantor moves assets into an irrevocable trust, those assets are subject to the gift tax. Depending on the terms of the trust (as discussed next), the trust may qualify for the $17,000 annual gift tax exclusion.

Gift in Trust – Crummey Trust

A donor can create a trust to give a gift that exceeds the annual exclusion limit, and without paying the gift tax. This is usually accomplished through a Crummey trust, which allows a beneficiary to withdraw assets within a limited period of time, such as three months. This arrangement gives the beneficiary a present interest in the trust, which qualifies the payment as a non-taxable gift.

A Crummey trust is intended for the receipt of gifts in a manner that qualifies them for exclusion from the gift tax. These arrangements are routinely used by parents in order to set up their children with lifetime gifts while still sheltering the assets from gift taxes. However, a gift's value within this arrangement cannot exceed the permitted annual exclusion amount, which is $17,000. As just noted, a Crummey trust gives the beneficiary a present interest in a gift. The trust achieves this by giving the beneficiary immediate access to the gifted assets (though not if they are a minor), though only up to the amount of the annual exclusion. The beneficiary cannot access the other funds in the trust until the next year, after which he or she can access the permitted annual exclusion amount again – and so on.

Gifts to Minors

A parent or grandparent might want to make a gift to a minor, such as a child or grandchild. The best tax protection for these gifts is based on the Uniform Gifts to Minors Act (UGMA), which allows individuals to transfer assets to minors. The UGMA allows a custodian to hold cash and securities for a minor until adulthood.

Transferred assets can be placed in a UGMA account, which is designed to hold assets for the beneficiary. Transfers into a UGMA account of up to $17,000 can be made per person per year that are free of the gift tax. Transfers into a UGMA account are irrevocable – which means that they are permanently owned by the beneficiary. The custodian of a UGMA account can be the donor, another person, or a financial institution. Whoever takes on the role of custodian has a fiduciary duty to oversee the account in the best interests of the beneficiary. A custodian can use the funds in the account to purchase stocks, bonds, mutual funds, and other securities on behalf of the beneficiary, though there is a limitation on investments in speculative instruments such as derivatives.

The assets placed in a UGMA account are typically used to pay for a minor's education, but the custodian can make withdrawals for almost any expenditures that can benefit the minor. There is no withdrawal penalty when funds are removed from a UGMA.

Tip: UGMA assets are owned by the beneficiary, which means that they count as assets when the minor applies for college financial aid. This can reduce a minor's eligibility for such aid.

Once minors reach adulthood, they are given full access to their UGMA account, which allows them to use the funds in any way they want.

Another gifting option is covered by the Uniform Transfers to Minors Act (UTMA). A custodial account set up under the UTMA can contain any kind of tangible or intangible asset, such as intellectual property, real estate, and works of art.

> **Note:** The assets stored in a UTMA account are counted as part of the custodian's estate until the targeted beneficiary reaches adulthood and takes possession.

Gifts that Appreciate in Value

It can make sense to gift property to someone now, if you think that there is a strong possibility of it appreciating in value in the future. Doing so pushes the asset out of your estate now, thereby reducing the value of your estate at a later date.

EXAMPLE

Evelyn owns farmland near a rapidly-growing city. She suspects that developers will start contacting her in a few years to buy the property and build residences on it, at which point the value of the farmland is likely to increase by several multiples of its current price. If she waits to transfer this property to her son Evan through her will, the property value may already have escalated, possibly resulting in an estate tax liability. Instead, she elects to gift the property to Evan now. Doing so keeps all subsequent appreciation out of her estate. This gift will likely result in some gift tax being paid, but this amount will be well below the estate tax that her estate would otherwise have to pay at a later date.

It makes less sense to gift property to someone that has already appreciated in value, since the recipient will receive your cost basis – which may be quite low in relation to its current market value. It makes more sense to transfer these assets following your death, when the recipient's basis in the assets will be their market value on the date of your death.

EXAMPLE

Monique acquired 500 shares in a pharmaceutical company for $20 a share. Following the release of several blockbuster drugs, the value of the shares has increased to $200. If Monique were to give the shares to her son Russell now, his cost basis in the shares would be $20, which would eventually result in a large taxable gain if he were to ever sell the shares. Conversely, if Monique were to leave the shares to Russell in her will, then he would obtain a stepped-up basis of $200 per share upon her death. If Russell were to then sell the shares for $200 each, his higher cost basis would result in no taxable gain at all.

IRS Form 709

Gift tax information is reported on IRS Form 709, *United States Gift Tax Return*. It is filed by the donor (the party issuing the gift). When a donor gives a gift that exceeds either the annual or lifetime exclusion amount, he or she must complete the form and include it as part of their annual income tax return. If all gifts made did not exceed the annual $17,000 exclusion, then there is no need to file the form. However, when spouses use gift splitting to gift an amount that exceeds $17,000, then each one must file the form (there is no joint gift tax return). If both spouses agree to split their gifts, both individual gift tax returns should be filed together in the same envelope, in order to help the IRS process the returns.

EXAMPLE

Alberto pays $17,000 in cash to his niece and $12,000 to his daughter. There is no requirement for repayment, so these payments are classified as gifts. Since the amounts paid do not exceed the annual exclusion amount, Alberto does not need to file Form 709.

EXAMPLE

Francis contributes $60,000 to his favorite charity, Hot Dogs for the Poor. This charity is classified by the IRS as a nonprofit, so the payment is classified as a charitable contribution. Since this payment is a gift, there is no need to file Form 709.

EXAMPLE

Zachary gifts an antique stove valued at $25,000 to his fiancé, Yvette. Zachary will have to file a Form 709, because the value of the gift is well over the annual exclusion amount. Also, the marital transfer exclusion does not apply, since they are not married at the time of the transfer.

Filing the form does not necessarily mean that any gift tax must be paid. For example, if a donor gives a gift that is greater than the $17,000 annual exclusion cap but which is under the $12.92 million lifetime exclusion cap, then no tax is paid.

> **Note:** The recipient of a gift does not have to complete this form, unless this party chooses to pay the gift tax on behalf of the donor.

Summary

The gift tax is levied by the federal government on gifts made to other persons, where the donor is required to pay the tax. The rules behind the tax have been constructed to minimize the number of instances in which the typical person will be required to pay it. The numerous exemptions from the rule encourage the ongoing gifting of smaller amounts, while a large lifetime exclusion essentially means that the tax is only triggered by extremely large gifts.

Chapter 13
Trust Concepts

Introduction

A trust is a fiduciary relationship in which the grantor gives the trustee the right to hold title to property or assets on behalf of a beneficiary. It is an essential concept in estate planning, as we will cover in the following pages.

Continuing Trusts

A *continuing trust* is one that lasts beyond the life of the person who created it. Therefore, the assets of the trust are not distributed immediately upon the death of the person establishing it, but rather they are distributed at some later date, as set forth in the relevant trust documentation. Such a trust can be created in a living trust or a will, or it may be initiated separately by the grantor. It is usually initiated through a living trust, in order to avoid probate. A continuing trust is irrevocable, and is intended to impose long-term controls over designated property. An ancillary reason for a continuing trust is to minimize estate taxes.

The terms of a continuing trust can be changed up to the point when it takes effect, after which it becomes irrevocable. This means that most people who use such a trust do not want it to take effect until they have died. Another good reason for a continuing trust not to take effect until your death is that any property placed in it prior to your death is considered a gift, and so is subject to gift tax.

> **Note:** You can only impose control over assets that are being set aside for people who are alive when you die. This rule keeps people from tying up property for extremely long periods of time.

Once a continuing trust goes into operation (usually triggered by the death of the grantor), the trustee has to obtain a taxpayer identification number for the trust, file annual income tax returns for it, and maintain an adequate set of supporting accounting records. The trustee then manages the property as set forth in the trust document, which may address such matters as when it is allowable to sell property and the conditions under which to acquire additional property. The trust continues in operation until a specific date is reached or a triggering event occurs, such as the death of the surviving spouse or a child reaching the age of 30.

> **Tip:** The work of a trustee can be substantial, especially when there are many assets involved. In this case, it might be sensible for the trustee to hire financial advisors to assist in making decisions about investing assets in a prudent manner.

The trustee is also in charge of distributing trust assets to the designated beneficiaries, as authorized by the trust document. When the trust ends, the trustee also handles the final distribution of assets to beneficiaries.

> **Tip:** It is quite common for the trustee of a continuing trust to be paid. It is not fair to expect this person to work for free, and you might reasonably suspect the motives of someone who *is* willing to work for free.

If you cannot find anyone competent who is willing to take on the trustee role, consider a private trust company. Their fees will certainly pile up, reducing the value of the trust property, but their competency level tends to be high. It may also be worthwhile to name a successor trustee, in case your initial choice is no longer able or willing to do the work.

Most people do not need a continuing trust. However, it can be useful in cases where you think the targeted beneficiary would be a spendthrift, or is a minor, or is disabled and therefore needs long-term support.

EXAMPLE

Phyllis, age 55, has a son, age 25, who is completely unable to handle money. She wants to leave him several million dollars in cash, but is concerned that he will spend it at once. To mitigate this risk, she creates a continuing trust within her living trust, which will be activated when she dies. The cash designated for her son will be transferred to the ongoing trust without going through probate. The trustee of the continuing trust will then oversee disbursements made by the trust to her son.

An ongoing trust can be useful when configured as a charitable trust, where property placed in the trust is designated to be for charitable purposes. This trust is operational and irrevocable as soon as you have signed off on the trust documentation.

AB Disclaimer Trusts

Another type of trust is the *AB trust*, where the trust can be split into two parts, which are Trust A and Trust B. It is designed for married couples, where each spouse creates his or her own AB trust. When the first spouse dies, his or her AB trust converts into an A trust, for which the surviving spouse becomes the life beneficiary. The survivor is then entitled to all income from the A trust, as well as to use the property in the trust, and to spend the Trust A principal for basic needs (including health care, education, support, and maintenance). The surviving spouse does not own the property in the Trust A, which instead goes to the final beneficiaries named by the deceased spouse when the surviving spouse eventually dies. All of the Trust A property is classified as being within the deceased spouse's estate, and is subject to that person's estate tax exemption. The surviving spouse's trust then becomes a B trust.

EXAMPLE

Joshua and Colleen have been married for many years, and have a son, Andy. They each create an AB trust. Joshua dies, so his property goes into Trust A, which means that Colleen's property goes into a revocable Trust B. Colleen is the life beneficiary of Trust A, and can use this property until she dies. Andy is the final beneficiary of Joshua, so all residual property in Trust A will eventually go to him.

Joshua's estate is valued at $5 million, so all of the trust property is eligible for his personal estate tax exemption. For the purpose of calculating estate tax, none of Joshua's estate is combined with the estate of Colleen.

Who would benefit from an AB trust? It can be used by high net worth couples that want to reduce their estate tax by keeping the property of the first-to-die spouse out of the estate of the remaining spouse.

A variation on the AB trust concept is the AB disclaimer trust. Under this arrangement, each spouse leaves the majority of their property to the other spouse, stating that any property disclaimed by the survivor goes into Trust A. When one spouse dies, the surviving spouse can either accept or disclaim the property of the deceased spouse. The survivor can decide how much of this trust property to officially inherit, and how much to put into the Trust A. Also, as is the case with any AB trust, the survivor gets use of the property remaining in Trust A, but does not own it.

An AB disclaimer trust is usually combined with a living trust, so that property avoids probate. This means that a trustee should be chosen, both for the living trust and the Trust A that begins when the first spouse dies. Usually, the surviving spouse is designated as the trustee for Trust A. Since it is not possible to tell which spouse will be the surviving spouse, both of them are designated as the trustee in the trust documents. It can be useful to also name an alternate successor trustee, in case the surviving spouse is unable to take on the trustee role.

EXAMPLE

Heather and Darren have four children and a combined estate worth $15 million. They set up an AB disclaimer trust in which both spouses are the designated trustees. Heather dies, so Darren becomes the sole trustee. He elects to disclaim some of Heather's assets, so Trust A is created for those assets. Darren becomes the trustee of that trust.

The AB disclaimer trust approach gives the surviving spouse the option to disclaim the other spouse's property, which can be useful in case the tax law subsequently changes. However, using this approach requires additional record keeping for the property stored in Trust A, and will require the filing of a separate tax return for the trust. Also, there is a risk of some conflict between the surviving spouse and the final beneficiaries, since the surviving spouse could end up using most (or all) of the trust principal to which the final beneficiaries would otherwise be entitled.

> **Tip:** AB trusts are complicated documents, so always hire an experienced attorney to write them for you.

QTIP Trusts

Under a *QTIP trust* arrangement[6], a married person names the surviving spouse as the life beneficiary of the property within the trust. When the surviving spouse eventually dies, the property passes to the final beneficiaries designated by the first spouse. Under this arrangement, when the first spouse dies, all of the property in the trust is exempt from estate tax, but is included in the surviving spouse's estate for estate tax purposes when the survivor dies. In addition, the surviving spouse receives all of the income from the property parked in the trust, and can require the trustee to convert all non-income producing assets into ones that produce income. The assets included in the QTIP do not go through probate following the death of the surviving spouse. This approach is used to delay the payment of estate taxes, thereby leaving more cash available for the surviving spouse. It is especially useful when both spouses have assets that exceed the estate tax threshold. In effect, a QTIP makes it look as though the surviving spouse had inherited from the deceased spouse using the marital deduction, while giving the deceased spouse control over the property and who will inherit it. This approach is most commonly used when one spouse is significantly older and wealthier than the other spouse and wants to provide for the younger spouse, while also leaving assets for the children from an earlier marriage.

EXAMPLE

Bill is 70 years old and married to Leila, who is 45 years old. Bill has assets worth $20 million, while Leila has very few assets. Leila will likely outlive Bill. Bill wants to ensure that Leila has sufficient funds to maintain a decent lifestyle when he is gone, but he also wants to leave significant assets for his three children from a prior marriage. Accordingly, he sets up a QTIP trust that contains all of his assets. The trust will be activated when he dies. Under its terms, Leila will be the life beneficiary (receiving all income from the assets), while his children are designated as the final beneficiaries, receiving all remaining assets after Leila dies.

The grantor has the option to give the surviving spouse control over how much each beneficiary actually inherits. This approach is used when the surviving spouse may live substantially longer than the grantor, and so is in a better position to determine who actually needs the money. This approach should only be used when the grantor absolutely trusts the surviving spouse to make the correct allocation decisions.

A potential downside of a QTIP trust is that the value of the property in the trust may increase during the remaining lifetime of the surviving spouse, which increases the amount of the estate tax that must be paid. This differs from the situation with an AB trust, where the value of the property in the trust is only determined as of the date of death of the grantor spouse.

---

[6] A QTIP trust is short for a Qualified Terminable Interest Property Trust.

EXAMPLE

Amy creates a QTIP trust that includes $15 million of property. Her husband Gregory dies 10 years later, at which point the value of the property in the trust has increased to $18 million. This $18 million property valuation is used to calculate Gregory's taxable estate.

Charitable Trusts

A charitable trust can be used to make a gift to a charity, and is a common giving tool for making larger contributions. It is a useful approach when you want to minimize either income taxes or estate taxes, and can also be set up to provide income for loved ones for the remainder of their lives before the underlying principal is turned over to a charity.

The type of charitable trust used depends on the particular blend of financial goals that you want to achieve. The main types of trusts are the charitable lead trust and the charitable remainder trust. *A charitable lead trust* is structured to pay out a portion of its income to a charity (which is the income beneficiary), with the remainder being paid to one or more beneficiaries when the trust is terminated. The donor receives an income tax deduction for the estimated value of the income donated to the charity. This deduction is spread over several years. However, the donor must pay income tax on all income received by the charity, which can offset the tax deduction.

It is useful to donate appreciated assets to this type of trust, in order to avoid incurring any capital gains tax. This approach is usually only used by very wealthy people, who own extremely appreciated assets that they want to retain within the family.

There are two types of charitable lead trusts, as outlined in the following bullet points:

- *Unitrust*. Pays out a fixed percentage of trust assets to a charity over a period of time. This requires annual reappraisals of trust assets, to determine the amount of the payout to the charity.
- *Annuity trust*. Pays out a fixed dollar amount to a charity each year.

EXAMPLE

Celina is a wealthy entrepreneur who has made millions from her chain of home improvement stores. Celina has three children from a previous marriage. She elects to create a charitable lead trust, which is funded with securities that she purchased many years ago for $50,000, and which are now worth $3,000,000. The income beneficiary is a cancer research institute. Celina sets the income payments to be made annually to the institute at 6% of the trust assets. Once Celina dies, the trust assets will be transferred to her children.

Celina avoids the massive capital gains tax that she would have incurred if she had sold the securities, while the charity incurs no tax liability on the sale. Celina can also take an income tax deduction on the income transferred to the institute, but will also have to pay income tax on these transfers. Finally, her children will receive all remaining trust assets when she dies.

A *charitable remainder trust* designates an income beneficiary and a final beneficiary, where the final beneficiary must be a charity. The income beneficiary is commonly the donor or that person's spouse, but can be anyone at all. This beneficiary receives payments from the trust for a period of time, such as all income from the trust assets during the person's life, or perhaps a fixed percentage of the remaining amount of trust assets each year. The income beneficiary does not own the trust assets, so they are not included in his or her estate. The donor receives an income tax deduction for the estimated value of the gift to the charity, minus the value of the payments that the income beneficiary will receive. This deduction is spread over several years. Also, under a charitable remainder trust arrangement, the charity that is the final beneficiary usually acts as the trustee, and so is responsible for making periodic payments to the income beneficiary.

There are several types of charitable remainder trusts, as outlined in the following bullet points:

- *Charitable remainder annuity trust.* Pays a fixed annual amount to the income beneficiary. If earnings from the trust assets are not sufficient, then the principal will be used to ensure that the fixed amount is paid, which can result in a significantly lower contribution to the charity. Once the trust is created, it is not possible to subsequently add more assets to the trust.
- *Charitable remainder unitrust.* Pays a percentage of trust assets to the income beneficiary each year. This approach requires a reappraisal of trust assets each year in order to determine the payout. It can provide a hedge against inflation, since the value of trust assets may increase in an inflationary period.
- *Charitable gift annuity.* Similar to an annuity trust, where the trust agreement sets forth the amount of income that the income beneficiary will receive each year. It is common to donate appreciated stock through this device, to avoid paying capital gains tax.
- *Pooled income trust.* Involves a donation to a charity, which then aggregates the donation with funds donated by other parties, and then manages the funds in one large trust. Interest on the invested funds is then paid back to the donors. Tangible property cannot be given to a pooled income trust. Obviously, the charity must always be the trustee, since it is managing the underlying pooled trust. This approach works well when you want to keep adding assets to the trust over time. It is common to donate appreciated stock through this device, to avoid paying capital gains tax.

EXAMPLE

Allen works for himself and earns a significant income. He is now 65 years old, is not married, and has no close relatives. A large part of his $10 million net worth is from an initial $1 million investment in a startup company. The firm has grown, increasing the value of his holdings, but it does not pay out any dividends. If Allen were to sell these shares and use the funds to buy other securities that pay out a regular dividend, he would have to pay capital gains tax on the resulting profit. He can avoid this issue by forming a charitable remainder unitrust where he is the income beneficiary, and a children's hospital is the final beneficiary.

By taking this step, Allen avoids paying tax on the profit earned from selling the startup company's shares. In addition, Allen specifies that he wants to be paid 5% of the trust assets per year, for the rest of his life. He can also take an income tax deduction on the estimated value of the gift to the children's hospital, minus the value of the payments that he will receive from the trust.

EXAMPLE

Timothy is a well-paid software developer, aged 35. He is not married and has no children. He wants to support a charity that provides medical services during catastrophes. He contributes $15,000 to a pooled fund managed by the charity, and takes an income tax deduction for the donation. He keeps doing this year after year, with the amount varying each year in accordance with his income level. By the time he is 65 years old, the amount managed by the trust has swelled to $625,000. He will receive the annual earnings generated from this investment. By taking this approach, Timothy has given a substantial amount to a favorite charity, while also setting up a series of retirement payments for himself.

Note: If payments are made to a third party by a charitable remainder trust, these payments are subject to the gift tax, so be aware that the trust may have to pay gift tax to the government, if the amount paid exceeds the annual gift tax exemption.

Tip: If the charitable organization is a large one, it probably has an investment staff with experience in managing charitable trusts, so it makes sense to designate the organization as the trustee. It can also provide assistance in preparing the relevant trust documents.

In both cases, the intent is to gift funds to a charity, while also providing income to someone, usually during their final years. In both cases, these charitable trusts are irrevocable; once they are set up, the donor cannot regain control over the underlying property. Also in both cases, the value of the charitable gift paid out is tax-deductible, but this is only the case when the charity has been approved by the IRS as being a tax-deductible 501(c)(3) entity; if not, then there are no tax benefits to be gained from the arrangement.

A particular advantage of using charitable donations is the donation of appreciated property through a charitable remainder trust, since you can avoid paying tax on the gain in value. The concept is best illustrated with an example. Suppose that you have a painting that you bought for $1,000, and which is now worth $1,000,000. You can donate the painting to a charity, which then sells it and uses the $1,000,000 to acquire securities that pay dividends. The charity does not pay any tax on the gain in value of the painting, and you can take a $1,000,000 tax deduction on its current fair value. In addition, the charity is now obligated to send you periodic dividend payments on the $1,000,000 that it realized from the sale of the painting. If you had sold the painting yourself and invested in the same securities, you would have earned a reduced dividend amount, because you would have had to pay capital gains tax on the increase in value of the painting.

A tangential advantage of using a charitable trust is that you can usually direct how a charity can use the funds sent to it. For example, a donor could specify that an educational institution receiving her donation use the cash to enhance its teaching facilities, or perhaps to provide scholarships to needy students.

A disadvantage of a charitable trust is that the receiving charity may insist on being the trustee. If so, and you are relying on it to provide you or a loved one with a reasonable annual income for a period of time, then there is a risk that the trust assets will be mismanaged – which can impact the amount of income received. If you have any concerns about the professionalism of the charity's staff, then do not designate that organization as the trustee. Either donate your assets to a different organization, or arrange to have a more professional trustee oversee the assets. Another concern is that the charity could lose its tax-deductible charity designation, in which case you will lose the related income tax deduction. To guard against this possibility, consider naming a backup charity with the proper tax-deductible IRS status, that will take over the trust assets.

Generation-Skipping Trusts

A *generation-skipping trust* operates as the name implies. It is set up to provide income to the second generation (your children), while leaving the trust principal to the third generation (your grandchildren). Someone in the second generation of beneficiaries usually acts as the trustee. This approach is intended to avoid estate taxes when the second generation dies, because that generation never owns the underlying trust assets. Instead, the estate tax burden falls on the third generation, when they die. This tax break is capped at the amount of the current generation-skipping transfer tax exemption. This concept is heavily used by very wealthy people, who are the most likely to pay estate taxes.

EXAMPLE

Gary has three children and five grandchildren. He creates a generation-skipping trust and parks $20 million of assets in it. The trust will take effect upon his death. Under the terms of the trust, his three children will receive all income from the trust during their lifetimes. When the children die, their estates do not pay estate tax on the trust assets, because they never owned the assets. At that point, all trust assets are delivered to the five grandchildren.

Note: A generation-skipping trust is not limited to your direct descendants. It can be applied to any situation in which you have beneficiaries in two subsequent generations.

Whenever there is a gift of trust property that skips a generation, the generation-skipping transfer tax is imposed. This tax is applied when the final beneficiaries receive these assets, which typically occurs only after the second generation has died. This tax is also applied when assets are gifted to someone two or more generations down. A generation skipping-trust is evaluated to see if it is subject to this tax when the grantor dies; if the amount in the trust at that time is less than the exempt amount, then the tax is not applied. Later, when the property in the trust is distributed to the third generation beneficiaries, the tax will not be applied – even if the value of the trust assets have subsequently increased. The following example provides additional information about the tax.

EXAMPLE

Wallace leaves $20 million to a grandchild, Susan. The exemption portion of the tax is applied to this gift, after which the remainder is taxed at the highest estate tax rate. In addition, the entire amount of this gift is included in Wallace's estate, and so is subject to the estate tax when Wallace dies. This means that the gifted property is taxed twice.

Irrevocable Life Insurance Trust

If you have a life insurance policy, then the proceeds from it will be included in the valuation of your estate when you die. If the policy is for a large amount, this may mean that some estate tax will be owed. To avoid estate tax, consider including the policy in an irrevocable life insurance trust. As the name implies, you will have no control over the trust once it has been set up, which also means that you cannot be trustee. This trust owns the life insurance policy, so the proceeds from the policy are excluded from your estate. Instead, the proceeds are paid out to the designated beneficiaries. This can be a particularly useful approach when the beneficiary is a minor, in which case the trustee can be instructed to maintain control over the funds until the minor becomes an adult.

Note: The proceeds from an irrevocable life insurance trust will only be excluded from your estate if it was established at least three years prior to your death.

Spendthrift Trust

When a beneficiary is likely to squander any funds left to him or her, the answer may be a *spendthrift trust*. For example, a beneficiary might be tempted to spend a large amount of cash on drugs or alcohol. In this case, property is allocated to a spendthrift trust, which is managed by someone other than the beneficiary. The trustee is responsible for making considered disbursements to the beneficiary, typically to cover basic living requirements, as directed by the trust document. If the beneficiary wastes even these funds, then the trustee can be empowered to cut off all disbursements – in this case, the trust document might allow the trustee to pay a different beneficiary.

In this situation, the job of the trustee is extremely difficult, having to determine which requests from the beneficiary are valid and which should be turned down. To make matters easier, consider including in the trust document a list of specific actions by the beneficiary that would warrant cutting off all further payouts. For example, a legal conviction involving jail time could be a trigger to switch to an alternate beneficiary.

Another option is to direct the trustee to make payments directly to third parties on behalf of the beneficiary, such as his or her landlord, so that the beneficiary has no opportunity to misuse trust assets.

The trust document should state when the trust will terminate. Typically, the trust terminates only later in the beneficiary's life, perhaps when the person is 40, 50, or even 60 years old.

The Power of Appointment

A key element in a trust arrangement is the *power of appointment*, which is the power to determine how your assets will be distributed following your death. For example, Zara authorizes her brother Emilio to distribute her remaining assets among her three children. If Emilio dies before her, then Zara gives the power of appointment to her sister Anita. Emilio or Anita are given the power to decide when the children will receive assets from her estate, depending on their life choices.

It is especially useful to use the power of appointment when there is some uncertainty about who your beneficiaries will be, and how much they will receive. However, given the decision-making power of the responsible party, this power should only be given to people in whom you have a very high level of trust. If there is any uncertainty about how the power will be used, it may be better to use a limited power of appointment. Under a limited power arrangement, the recipient of this power cannot receive any assets from your estate. Further, a limited arrangement designates exactly which beneficiaries can receive assets.

EXAMPLE

Jim and Doris have four children. Jim dies first. In his AB trust, he gives Doris a limited power of appointment to direct how the trust assets will eventually be distributed among the children. Doris lives another 15 years, during which time she notes that one child suffers severely from a car accident, requiring substantial home care, while the other three turn out to be quite successful. Doris exercises her limited power of appointment by leaving 90% of the trust property to the injured child, with the remaining 10% of the assets being distributed equally among the other three children.

Summary

When deciding whether to set up a trust, be aware that there are significant tradeoffs associated with these entities. If your goal is to avoid estate taxes or shield property from creditors, that may be possible – but at the price of losing control over the assets. In short, you have to give something up in order to gain tax advantages through a trust, and you might not like that loss of control.

Chapter 14
Disclaimer Options

Introduction

It is possible that a beneficiary will turn down (or disclaim) an inheritance. If so, the inheritance goes to a secondary beneficiary, or the residuary beneficiary. Why would anyone do this? Usually, it is because the beneficiary already has a substantial estate, and wants the assets to go to someone who is more in need. In this case, disclaiming the inheritance is better than accepting the assets, gifting them to the needier relatives, and then having to pay gift tax on these transfers. Also, a disclaimer can prevent a beneficiary's estate from becoming so large that it will now be subject to the estate tax.

EXAMPLE

Henry has two sons, Alton and Ruger. Henry has designated them to equally share in his estate, which is worth $500,000. Alton is well off, due to a series of high-paying jobs and discerning investments, and now has an estate worth $6 million. Ruger has had a more difficult time, having only accumulated a few thousand dollars. Alton decides that the inheritance would have a greater positive impact on Ruger, so he disclaims his share of the inheritance, resulting in all $500,000 going to Ruger.

EXAMPLE

John dies and leaves his estate (worth $5 million) to his brother Douglas. Douglas is nearly 80 years old and has an estate valued at $12 million, so he is just under the threshold at which estate taxes will be levied. The alternate beneficiary is a 35-year-old niece with few assets. If Douglas accepts the inheritance, his estate will eventually have to pay estate tax. He instead elects to disclaim the inheritance, so the $5 million is passed to the niece. The niece does not have enough assets for her estate to ever pay the inheritance tax, even with the $5 million added to it.

If the alternate beneficiary is someone in the next generation, then this presents another opportunity to disclaim an inheritance. By doing so, the inheritance passes straight through to a younger beneficiary who is more likely to need the assets. This is a particularly useful option when the primary beneficiary already owns substantial assets.

Disclaimer Rules

For a disclaimer to be valid, it must follow certain rules set forth by the IRS. These rules are as follows:

- The disclaimer must be contained within a written document.
- The disclaimer must be completed within nine months of the decedent's death.
- The beneficiary providing the disclaimer cannot already have taken any benefit from the property.
- The beneficiary can provide no instructions for how the property will be dispositioned.

In regard to the last point, the decedent's will or trust provides instructions regarding who will receive any disclaimed property.

Once written, the disclaimer is delivered to the decedent's executor or the trustee of the decedent's living trust.

Tip: Take as much of the nine-month period as you need in order to work through the monetary and tax implications of any possible disclaimers, before writing these documents.

Tip: It can be useful to include a discussion of disclaimers in your will or living trust, so that your beneficiaries are aware of the concept. It is then up to them if they want to take advantage of this option.

There can be a complication when you are the successor trustee of a living trust, and you stand to inherit property from the trust. If you also have the power to decide where disclaimed property goes, then you cannot disclaim it at all. If you were to disclaim the property in this situation, the IRS would classify the property as being part of your estate, and would charge a gift tax for any distributions made to other parties. The only ways out of this conundrum are to either decline the ability to direct how trust property is distributed, or resign from the trustee position.

Tip: If it seems possible that your successor trustee will have to resign to avoid the just-described situation, be especially carefully in designated an alternative successor trustee, since this person may very well end up being in charge of the trust.

Summary

The key issue with disclaimers is that so few beneficiaries know that this option even exists. Consequently, if your designated beneficiaries might be a position where they could elect to disclaim an inheritance, be sure to make note of this option in your will.

Chapter 15
Estate Planning for a Business

Introduction

For many business owners, the bulk of their wealth is tied to their business, rather than any personal assets they may own. If so, they need to consider estate planning that encompasses how the organization will be managed following their death, and the avoidance of both probate and estate taxes. We cover these issues in the following pages, along with the use of family partnerships to reduce the tax rate paid by the members of a family in aggregate.

Planning for Management of the Business

A key concern for a business owner is who will run it after his or her death. The best approach is to adopt a succession plan, where one or more people within the organization are groomed for the advanced level of responsibility associated with senior management roles. Then, in the event of your death, there will be a designated successor on the premises, and hopefully several others available as backups.

In some families, the succession plan focuses on bringing other family members into management positions. There can be several problems with these family succession arrangements. First, are the targeted people actually capable of taking over the owner's role? If not, putting them in charge could negatively impact the competitiveness of the entire business. In this case, it can make more sense to allow better-qualified people to take over senior management roles, even if they are not members of the family. Another concern is that co-owners may object to your insertion of a family member into a management position. When there are multiple owners, it can make sense to clearly state the succession plan in a formal document, such as a partnership or shareholders' agreement.

A variation on the future management of your business is the use of a buyout clause among the owners. This clause allows the other owners to buy out your share of the business in the event of your death. This can be structured as a right of first refusal, where they can buy your share at the price that an independent third party would be willing to pay. Or, the buyout clause can state the specific valuation method to be used, such as a multiple of the average cash flow level for the past few years.

> **Tip:** Pay particular attention to the duration and nature of buyout payments by the other business owners. A lengthy payment period increases the risk that delayed payments will never be paid, and also reduces the present value of the payments.

A common problem is when you have several children who will inherit your estate, but only one or two of them are interested in running the business. Some options are to leave the entire business to those children willing to run it, or to split ownership evenly among the entire group, and let those willing to run it receive generous pay from the business to compensate them for their efforts. The following example illustrates the problem.

EXAMPLE

David and Katherine run a highly profitable business that sells baby supplies. They believe in the mission of the business so much that they have jointly produced eight children. Unfortunately, only two of them are interested in running the business after David and Katherine die.

One solution is to leave their entire ownership interest in the business to the two children most interested in running it, but doing so will leave far fewer assets to distribute among the remaining six children. Another option is to evenly split the ownership interest among the eight children, while leaving all management decisions to the two children who will participate in the business. This latter approach seems more favorable, since it is most likely to increase the value of the business, which will favorably impact the net worth of all eight children.

Another common concern is when none of your children are interested in running the business, or none of them appear to have the management skill to do so. If so, the best remaining option may well be to sell the firm to a third party. However, selling it immediately after your death may give the appearance of being a fire sale, resulting in low prices being offered for it. An alternative to consider is offering a few key employees a share in the proceeds from a sale. Doing so gives them an incentive to spruce up the business for sale, hopefully resulting in a higher valuation.

Estate Tax Reduction Tactics

When you own a business, a major concern is whether estate taxes will be so large that your heirs will be forced to sell the business in order to come up with the necessary funds. This is only an issue if the deceased person's net assets exceed the current year's estate tax exemption. This exemption is substantial, so estate taxes will likely not be an issue for most smaller businesses.

If estate tax is due, an option worth considering is to pay it to the IRS in installments over 14 years. Doing so may allow those inheriting the business to retain their ownership of it, thereby allowing them to use subsequent cash flows from the business to pay the taxes. Under this arrangement, the IRS will charge a modest interest rate, but the extended nature of the payments makes it an attractive option.

Another option is to give away minority interests in the business to other family members, such as your children. The value of such a gift is reduced when it is a minority interest, because it does not give the recipient control over the business. The valuation of this discount should be left to an appraiser, since the resulting appraisal report can be used as a defense if the IRS questions the valuation.

EXAMPLE

Alvin Finchley is the owner of Finchley Fireworks, which has 100,000 shares of stock outstanding. According to his CPA, these shares would sell for $50 each. However, if the shares were to be split between minority and majority shareholders, the minority shares would be valued at a 30% discount, resulting in a valuation of $35 per share. Alvin leaves 20,000 shares to each of his two sons. For the purpose of calculating gift tax, these shares are valued at $35 each. The IRS would likely consider this discount to be reasonable, and so would allow the $35 valuation for the purpose of calculating gift tax.

See the gift taxes chapter for more information about the gift tax exemption.

Probate Avoidance

It is essential for a business to avoid being tied up in the probate process, since it will be placed under court control for an extended period of time. This state of affairs can be troublesome, since court approval will be needed for a broad range of business decisions. A living trust, as described earlier in this book, is a good way to avoid enmeshing your business in probate. A living trust essentially transfers ownership of the business directly to your heirs. In cases where you want to leave interests in your business to multiple heirs, a good way to do so is to incorporate and then transfer ownership of the resulting shares into a living trust. The shares can then be apportioned among the heirs.

Family Partnerships

A sole proprietor may elect to form a partnership with other members of his or her family. If these new partners are being taxed at lower marginal income tax rates, then the aggregate result is a substantial reduction in the income taxes paid by the family as a whole. In short, some of the partnership's income is being shifted to family members with lower incomes, and who therefore pay a lower income tax rate. Given the tax advantages of this approach, the IRS is particularly watchful to see if any shares of partnership income are being routed to low-income partners who provide minimal service to the partnership. In particular, the IRS may impose the parent's marginal income tax rate on any partnership income allocated to a child, unless it can be proven that the child provided services to the partnership in exchange for the allocated income. Similarly, a purported gift of a partnership interest may be ignored if, in substance, the donor continues to own the interest through his or her power to control or influence the recipient's business decisions.

The IRS will recognize a family member as a partner in either of the following circumstances:

- When capital is a material income-producing factor in the partnership, and a family member acquires this capital interest in a legitimate transaction, such as by purchasing it or as a received gift; or
- When capital is not a material income-producing factor, but a family member is providing substantial services to the partnership.

Summary

An ownership interest in a family-run business can be a substantial asset, and the chief source of the family's wealth. This means that any estate planning relating to the business should not be taken lightly. Your best option is to consult with an estate planning specialist regarding all available options, and to periodically return to that person for additional discussions as the nature of the business changes over time.

Chapter 16
Planning for Personal Incapacity

Introduction

It is possible that you will have physical or mental problems prior to your death that will render you incompetent to make certain decisions. If so, several arrangements can be made to ensure that you are taken care of during any period of personal incapacity. We cover these options in the following pages.

Planning for Personal Incapacity

One way to deal with personal incapacity issues is to not plan for them at all. If so, and you later become incapacitated, then a judge will appoint a guardian to make decisions on your behalf. This approach is not recommended, since the associated court time is expensive, as are the ongoing fees charged by the guardian – which can cut substantially into your estate. In addition, anything stated during court proceedings will generally be public knowledge, which may not be a desirable state of affairs.

A better option is to set up legally valid documents that direct how your affairs should be handled in the event of your incapacitation. For example, you can specify what medical actions are to be taken in the event of an injury or medical condition. In particular, you can specify whether you want to receive life-prolonging treatments when the resulting quality of life will be low, or whether these treatments are to be withheld. In addition, you can specify who is authorized to make these decisions. Further, you can specify who will handle your finances, and provide this person with direction regarding how assets are to be invested and what expenditures to authorize. This person can deal with such matters as using your assets to pay for ongoing expenses, pay taxes, invest excess funds, manage your retirement accounts, and so forth.

> **Note:** If you can communicate your wishes in any way, then any legal documents concerning medical or financial decisions are not activated. They are only activated when you are in a permanent coma.

Planning for personal incapacity is especially important when the members of your family have differing opinions about what to do. To avoid rifts within the family over these decisions, take the matter away from them by preparing legally valid controlling documents.

Health Care Directives

In most states, you should prepare two documents that allow you to specify the nature of your medical care, both of which are classified as health care directives. The first is a declaration (also known as a *living will*), which is intended for medical personnel, and which identifies the medical care that you want to receive, as well as the medical care you do *not* want to receive in the event of your incapacitation. This document is targeted at whether you want to receive expensive and possibly painful treatments that may only prolong your life for a short period of time. Medical personnel should either follow your directive or transfer you to someone who will do so.

> **Note:** Be sure to state in your living will whether you want to receive pain medication, since a directive to stop such medication could leave you in significant discomfort during a final illness.

In addition, you should create a durable power of attorney for health care, in which you designate someone to act on your behalf to ensure that medical personnel are giving you the medical care that you specified. This person may also be authorized to have a relatively broad authority to make decisions concerning the types of health care that you will receive. For example, this person might have the power to give or with-hold consent for certain medical procedures, hire or fire medical personnel, and obtain court authorizations when medical providers do not want to honor your wishes.

> **Note:** A do-not-resuscitate order states that you do not wish to be revived if your heart stops or you stop breathing. It must usually be signed by a doctor to be considered valid. It is also known as a DNR form or DNR directive. The form should be kept in an obvious location where emergency medical personnel can see it, such as on the front of your refrigerator.

EXAMPLE

Jeffrey has been ill for quite a long time, and now faces a major surgery that will likely inca-pacitate him for an extended period. He creates a durable power of attorney for health care, in which he delegates to his sister Dorothy the power to make medical decisions on his behalf. Jeffrey includes several conditions in this document, including a requirement that all surgery be conducted at Saint Mark's Hospital, with Dr. Anderson performing the surgery.

Depending on the state, health care directives are generally not valid until you sign them in the presence of witnesses, which may include a notary public. This require-ment is needed in order to prove that you were of sound mind when you created the documents.

> **Tip:** Review your health care directives every few years, to ensure that you agree with the wishes codified in the documents. If not, replace them with new versions. To make this replacement easier, maintain a listing of who has received copies of these docu-ments, so that their copies can be destroyed and replaced with the new versions.

A durable power of attorney for finances is used when you want a trusted person to take over your financial affairs while you are incapacitated. This document can be designed to take effect immediately, or only after a doctor certifies that you have been incapacitated. In the first case, the document goes into effect as soon as you sign it. In the second case, the document is known as a *springing power of attorney*, and only goes into effect when a party stated in the document decides that you are now incapacitated; this can involve obtaining a doctor's statement regarding your incapacity. A springing power of attorney document can be difficult to construct, so have an attorney write it for you.

A durable power of attorney should be signed in the presence of a notary public, and possibly other witnesses (depending on state law). Otherwise, your agent may have difficulty getting third parties to accept him or her as your valid agent. Keep this document in a safe place where your agent can access it, since the document will be needed to obtain the cooperation of financial institutions.

Note: If a durable power of attorney for finances gives your agent power over real estate, then it must be filed in the land records office of the county in which your property is located.

Your Health Care Agent

The selection of a health care agent is a difficult one, for you are imposing a hard task on another person – deciding whether to give you certain types of medical care, which in turn may result in your death. This can be an especially troublesome task when there are multiple medical options to sort through, where the outcomes are not certain. The following points are worth considering when making the selection:

- Does the person live nearby? If so, it will be easier for the person to regularly travel to the hospital to monitor your condition.
- Does the person have enough fortitude to follow through with your wishes? This is a particular concern when some family members have alternative opinions about your treatment.
- Does the person have a reasonable knowledge of the medical procedures that might be involved? When this is the case, the agent will be able to compare the available options and make the best choice that matches your stated wishes.

Tip: Designate a backup agent, in case the primary agent is unable to serve.

It can make sense to give your power of attorney for financial matters to the same person who will be your health care agent. Otherwise, you may end up with two people who have difficulty working together to manage your affairs.

Tip: Unless your financial affairs are quite simple, it is generally prudent to allow the person handling your finances to receive a reasonable amount of compensation for his or her efforts on your behalf.

92

Summary

The capstone to planning for your personal incapacity is making sure that all health care directives are already in the hands of your doctor, agent, and at least one other party. Having these documents well distributed in advance limits the risk that no one will be able to find the documents when you are incapacitated.

Chapter 17
Actions to Take Following a Death

Introduction

What are the steps that a person should take when someone dies who has an estate plan? In this chapter, we summarize the actions to be taken, depending on a variety of estate planning scenarios.

When the Decedent Had a Will

When the decedent left a will, the person identified as the executor carries out the terms stated within the document. If some or all of the decedent's assets must go through probate, then the executor normally hires an attorney to handle these activities. Once the probate process has been completed, the executor then distributes the related assets to the beneficiaries named in the will.

If the will creates an ongoing trust, then the executor is typically named as the trustee, in which case this person will have ongoing responsibilities to oversee the trust assets.

If the will leaves assets to a minor, then the executor will transfer those assets to a designated custodian.

A key responsibility of the executor is to complete the decedent's final federal and state income tax returns. Depending on the complexity of these returns, the executor may want to hire a tax accountant to prepare the necessary documents.

When the Decedent Had a Living Trust

When the decedent left a living trust, the successor trustee named in the trust document must follow its instructions. Essentially, this means transferring all named trust property to the beneficiaries stated in the trust document. These actions can be taken as soon as the person dies. However, in the case of a couple, the surviving spouse serves as the trustee; the successor trustee only takes over after the second spouse dies.

When the living trust is for a single person, the successor trustee generally does not have to sell off trust property or manage it. Such activities are the responsibility of the beneficiaries who receive the property. Once all assets have been distributed, the trust automatically ends – there is no need to submit a formal trust termination document to anyone.

EXAMPLE

Frank's living trust states that his vacation home in Steamboat will be left to his three children. Following his death, the successor trustee deeds the property from the trust to the children. The children can then take whatever action they want with the house, such as selling it, renting it out, or using it as a vacation home. The successor trustee does not sell the house or manage the property.

While this settlement process might seem simple for the successor trustee, there are several additional steps to be taken. The trustee must obtain multiple copies of the decedent's death certificate[7], which will need to be submitted to a variety of third parties in order to obtain access to the decedent's assets. In addition, state law may require the trustee to fill out a form that gives the person legal authority to take actions on behalf of the trust, and file it with the state government. Finally, the trustee will need to obtain a professional appraisal of all real estate held within the trust, which is needed to provide beneficiaries with a stepped-up basis in the property to its market value on the decedent's date of death.

The situation is somewhat different when a living trust is associated with a couple. In this case, the successor trustee is (usually) initially the surviving spouse. This person must divide all property held within the trust into two parts, where new trust entities are created for the property of the deceased spouse and for the property of the surviving spouse. The property held in the trust for the deceased spouse is distributed to all designated beneficiaries right away, while the property held in the trust for the surviving spouse continues in operation. It is quite common for the trust property of the deceased spouse to be distributed to the surviving spouse, so there is little actual distribution of assets to third parties. Once all property has been distributed from the trust of the deceased spouse, that trust no longer exists. Once the surviving spouse eventually dies, the successor trustee stated in the trust documents becomes the trustee. This person distributes assets from the trust in the same manner as just described from the trust of a single individual.

In cases where property is left to a child, the assets are normally left in some variation on a child's trust. When this is the case, the successor trustee transfers the property to the designated manager of the child's trust. It is possible that the successor trustee is already tasked with both roles, in which case he or she must oversee the property until the terms of the trust mandate that the property be turned over to the child.

---

[7] A death certificate can be obtained from the mortuary that is responsible for the final disposition of the decedent's body. It may also be possible to obtain a death certificate from the applicable county health department. Another approach is to fill out an on-line form, if offered by the county where the death occurred (possibly contained within the Vital Records section of the website).

When the Decedent Had an Ongoing Trust

When the decedent left an ongoing trust, it is expected to run for an extended period of time, perhaps for multiple years. Given the duration of the trust arrangement, this is a much more complicated situation for the trustee, who must document exactly which assets are now in the trust, and ensure that all title documents state the trust as the owner of the assets. This trust will also need its own federal tax identification number, so that the trustee can file annual tax returns for the trust. In order to file tax returns, the trustee must also maintain an adequate system of accounting records. Furthermore, the trustee will need to make decisions about how to best utilize trust property in order to generate a reasonable level of income.

Multiple Trustee Situations

If several trustees are named in a living trust document, the alternate successor trustee will only take over when every person named as the primary successor trustee is unable to serve in this capacity.

If you are a designated successor trustee and are unable to serve in this capacity, then you can resign by signing a statement of resignation and delivering it to the person named as the alternate successor trustee. Depending on how the trust document is written, you may be able to appoint a new person as the successor trustee, if the trust document does not name anyone else. In this situation, your appointment document must be signed and notarized.

Tax Return Obligations

The executor of an estate is obliged to file final income tax returns on behalf of the decedent. Also, if the decedent's assets were substantial, then the executor will also have to file federal estate tax returns and state inheritance tax returns (if applicable). However, if the assets are held within a living trust, the successor trustee is responsible for filing these estate and inheritance tax returns (though the executor and successor trustee may be the same person).

Reports to Beneficiaries

A trustee usually does not have to report to beneficiaries about any trust activities, or the income generated by it. However, the terms of an ongoing trust might require the trustee to make such reports, such as sending them a copy of the trust's annual federal tax return. Also, a small number of states mandate that beneficiaries receive an annual report, for which the report contents vary by state.

Obtaining Joint Tenancy Title

When property is held in a joint tenancy arrangement, there are two owners, with the survivor automatically obtaining full ownership of the property upon the death of the other owner. In this situation, the surviving joint tenant will want to remove the other party's name from the applicable ownership document, such as the title to a car or a property deed. To do so, the survivor files a copy of the death certificate with the appropriate government department, and also files a statement that he or she is now the sole owner of the property. For example, to obtain sole title to joint tenancy real estate, these documents would be filed with the county recorder's office. This action can be taken without a lawyer, as it is fairly routine.

Collecting on Life Insurance Policies

One of the most common tasks for an executor is to collect on any outstanding life insurance policies. This is typically done by filling out a form provided by the insurer and submitting it back to the insurer, along with a certified copy of the decedent's death certificate. In some cases, the insurer may also require that the beneficiary submit a proof of identity before it will pay out any funds.

Glossary

A

AB trust. A trust that can be split into two parts, which are Trust A and Trust B. It is designed for married couples, where each spouse creates his or her own AB trust.

B

Beneficiary. Those who receive assets from trust property after the grantor dies.

C

Charitable lead trust. A trust that pays out a portion of its income to a charity, with the remainder being paid to one or more beneficiaries when the trust is terminated.

Charitable remainder trust. A trust that designates an income beneficiary and a final beneficiary, where the final beneficiary must be a charity.

Common property. The concept that a spouse who earns money and acquires property gets to own it.

Community property. The concept that property acquired or earned by each spouse during marriage is owned equally by each.

Continuing trust. A trust that lasts beyond the life of the person who created it.

D

Decedent. A person who has died.

E

Electronic will. A will that is created, signed, and stored online.

Estate tax. A tax levied on the net value of the estate of a deceased person before distribution to the heirs.

F

Family pot trust. When assets are left in a common pot for at least two children.

Final beneficiary. Someone who inherits a property outright.

Formal will. A properly typed, signed, and witnessed document that assigns assets to beneficiaries, and may also appoint an executor, as well as a guardian for any minors.

Future interest. When a beneficiary obtains a right to an asset, but which will be triggered at a future date.

G

Generation-skipping trust. A trust that is set up to provide income to the second generation (your children), while leaving the trust principal to the third generation (your grandchildren).

Gift tax. A federal tax that is imposed on a donor who gives something of value to another person while the donor is still living, where the donor gives up all control over the transferred asset.

Grantor. The person who sets up a trust.

J

Joint tenancy. When each owner owns an equal share of property. When the first owner dies, that person's share goes to the survivors.

Joint will. A will that has been created by two people (usually a married pair).

L

Life estate beneficiary. Someone who receives the right to use an asset or receive income from it during his or her lifetime, but who will not be its legal owner.

Life insurance. An insurance policy that pays out a sum of money following the death of an insured person.

Liquid asset. Any asset that is readily convertible into cash within a short period of time, and which suffers no loss in value as a result of the conversion.

Living trust. A legal document that lets you distribute your possessions to beneficiaries after you die.

Living will. A declaration that is intended for medical personnel, and which identifies the medical care that you want to receive, as well as the medical care you do *not* want to receive in the event of your incapacitation.

N

Net worth. Your assets minus liabilities.

P

Pour-over will. A will that directs that the assets subjected to it be transferred into a trust.

Power of appointment. The power to determine how your assets will be distributed following your death.

Present interest. When a beneficiary obtains an unrestricted right to the immediate use or enjoyment of an asset or the income derived from it.

Primary beneficiary. A party to whom you are leaving identified gifts.

Probate. The legal process of distributing a decedent's assets.

Q

QTIP trust. When a married person names the surviving spouse as the life beneficiary of the property within the trust. When the surviving spouse eventually dies, the property passes to the final beneficiaries designated by the first spouse.

R

Residuary beneficiary. Someone who receives assets that have not been specifically gifted to other beneficiaries.

S

Spendthrift trust. A trust that is intended to control the expenditures of a beneficiary, with a trustee responsible for all payouts from the trust.

Springing power of attorney. A power of attorney that only goes into effect when the party stated in the document decides that you are now incapacitated.

Statutory will. A standardized form in which you check a few boxes and fill in a few blanks in order to create a will.

T

Trust. A separate legal entity that owns assets, where a responsible party manages the assets.

Trust property. The assets transferred into a trust.

Trustee. Anyone who has control over a trust.

W

Will. A legal document in which is specified who receives your property when you die.

Index

www.ingramcontent.com/pod-product-compliance
Lightning Source LLC
Chambersburg PA
CBHW051224200326

41519CB00025B/7240